"My capability to tune into the energy of love gives me the words I need when I am ready to speak up, the compassion I need to forgive, and the power I need when I am lost."

- Gabrielle Bernstein, The Universe Has Your Back

Contents

guided by Love

A first aid kit
for your broken
heart

LINDSEY ELMS

ISBN:

978-1-916529-34-2 (Paperback)

978-1-916529-35-9 (ebook)

Cover design by Lynda Mangoro.

The Unbound Press
www.theunboundpress.com

Hey unbound one!

Welcome to this magical book brought to you by The Unbound Press.

At The Unbound Press we believe that when women write freely from the fullest expression of who they are, it can't help but activate a feeling of deep connection and transformation in others. When we come together, we become more and we're changing the world, one book at a time!

This book has been carefully crafted by both the author and publisher with the intention of inspiring you to move ever more deeply into who you truly are.

We hope that this book helps you to connect with your Unbound Self and that you feel called to pass it on to others who want to live a more fully expressed life.

With much love,

Nicola Humber

Founder of The Unbound Press

www.theunboundpress.com

Praise for Guided by Love

A REALLY PRACTICAL GUIDE

This book is something very special. The author gives a very personal account of heartbreak but gives the reader lots of opportunities to personalise this and make it relatable for them.

- Brian Miller

BEAUTIFUL AND HEARTFELT

This is such a beautiful book. I could feel in my heart how much love has been put into every single page and despite the pain endured how carefully every sentence was written. Lindsey ensures the person who is reading this book not only understands her personal story, they also take something magical for themselves. She has shared so much hope for anyone who holds it in their hands.

- Stella Tudor, Soul Alchemist

COMPASSIONATE AND INSIGHTFUL

A beautifully written book full of compassion and understanding. A very 'human' account of how to turn things around following difficult life experiences. I found 'Guided by Love' to be surprisingly uplifting... thank you, Lindsey Elms :-)

- Jan Porteous

BRILLIANT FIRST AID KIT

Brilliant guide to show how you can recover from a heartbreak, self-hatred or feeling low. The practical step by step guidance is easy to understand and try, including Nine Star Ki, game, journal, meditation, etc. The author's marriage breakup story and feelings can be related to any readers. Assuring and positive quotes are dotted around.

Thought-provoking and heartwarming short stories appear. You feel much better and think positive after reading this book.

- Kimie Horsman

DOES WHAT IT SAYS ON THE TIN

Really nicely written. There are so many memories of heart break and angst out there, this book is refreshingly the opposite. We get glimpses of the heartbreak that lead to the journey, but this is so much more. Simple guidance from the heart of a writer that found healing and wants to share her kit.

- Samantha Cottee

A ROAD MAP FOR YOUR JOURNEY TO RECOVERY

One stormy night Lindsey's world fell apart. This book is the remarkable story of how she rebuilt her life, seeking answers to the key questions: why and what happens next? Drawing upon her experiences of recovery she offers her readers a road map, a first aid kit of tools and processes with which those in despair can reconstruct their lives through love, compassion and self-care. I wholly commend this book to any reader who is looking for a guide to help them on their journey of recovery ¬ ¬ — they will not be disappointed.

- Steve Watts, CEO, Watts Coaching and Consulting Ltd, BEd (Hons) and MPhil

AN EXCEPTIONAL GUIDEBOOK

Arising from painful personal experience, Lindsey Elms' Guided by Love: A First-Aid Kit for Your Broken Heart offers a treasure chest of exercises, journaling, mantras, meditations, and other tools to go deeper into the wounded psyche and emerge radiant, whole, and transformed. Among the cycles that help the reader chart her course is 9 Star Ki, a universal cycle of energy flow with roots in the I Ching and Feng Shui astrology in China and the Nine Muses in Greek mythology. Lindsey's understanding of the soul and its web of intersecting paths to health, happiness, and wisdom make this an exceptional guidebook.

- Alex and Danka Jack, directors of Planetary Health, Inc. and teachers of 9 Star Ki

HEARTWARMING

"A wonderful heartwarming book, full of love and compassion. Highly recommended."

- Kelly Oliver-Dougall

Foreword

I am Mandy Nicholson, and I am a Creative Genius Consultant, Artist, Author, and Creative Retreat owner who helps creative women launch, grow and scale their businesses, and make more money.

I was lucky enough to meet Lindsey via the online space when she booked a Discovery Call with me and subsequently joined my Creative Mastermind program. Through working together on her business and spending time together during a retreat at my creative space in Scotland, we have built a special relationship.

Lindsey is a truly loving and kind soul who has a passion for helping others, so when she discussed writing this book, I was her biggest cheerleader.

I have seen the power of the help Lindsey offers to others through her holistic 9 Star Ki approach, coupled with her own intuitive and empathic skills. The personal journey of learning she has experienced through life's challenges has enhanced her ability to connect with and coach others. Her gentle and loving nature makes her a real joy to work with and this book is packed to the brim with her personal magic and genuine love for her fellow humans.

The pain of losing her marriage has enhanced her ability to help others face and deal with their pain. Learning to not only cope, but to thrive during such a difficult time has fine-tuned her skills and allowed her to create a wonderful first aid kit for those in pain from a broken heart.

Lindsey has written this book so beautifully; you can almost feel the love oozing from the pages. Her own journey is honestly portrayed and used incredibly well to demonstrate how others can navigate their pain. Her writing skills will take you on the journey with her. You will laugh, cry, smile and feel the hope and opportunity in every carefully crafted word.

What impresses me most, and I am sure will impress you, is Lindsey's thirst for knowledge and answers. They say knowledge is power and the consistent effort she had demonstrated around her subject is equivalent to a PhD in life (my opinion not a scientific fact!). You are in good and gentle hands when you are in Lindsey's world, absorb the lessons like she has and allow yourself to be healed.

My involvement in this book has been the best kind, I was asked to read it. I have watched Lindsey's journey, been there when she needed me and now had the privilege of being invited to read the book and write this foreword. My final comment to you, the reader is this...enjoy the gifts this book will bring into your life and immerse yourself in its pages. You won't regret it.

Mandy Nicholson BA, BSc

Preface

I sat in my car as the wind howled around me. I could hear trees falling and the rain battering my windscreen. It was pitch black and bitterly cold. Inside my car I was shivering; not only from the cold but also from the shock. My body reeling from the news, my heart breaking. I sat trying to shake it off like a bad dream. I thumped the steering wheel angrily, wailing, sobbing and despairing.

What was I going to do? How could this be happening?

It was the worst storm we had had in a decade. It was also the evening of my 20th Wedding Anniversary; the night my husband, out of the blue, told me he was leaving.

Waves of shock and panic rippled through me. My stomach felt like the inside of a washing machine spin cycle. The intensity of my feelings gained momentum as my heart pounded faster and faster, almost beating out of my chest.

The weather outside so obviously reflecting my internal emotions. The destruction of the storm echoing the destruction of my life.

The man I thought was my soul mate, who I would grow old and wrinkly with had decided to leave me, our kids, our home and move to the other end of the country. It may as well have been the other end of the world.

Of course, like every marriage we had our share of challenges, none though that I thought were insurmountable. Sometimes I forgot to do the washing up, sometimes he forgot to get a card. We had grown up together and our partnership had made us better people. Every day there was a check in call from him and I'd get a schoolgirl sense of excitement when his car pulled onto the drive.

This was the man I was so connected to that we simultaneously chose the same Christmas lights at different shops on the same evening.

Yet there he was shoving a few items of clothes into a bag, whilst I followed him around the house like a lost sheep trying to get him to talk to me, to make sense of what was going on. Him looking up at me with a teary blank face saying, *"I've made my choice, I just have to go."*

I felt my entire world crumble apart.

I had wanted so badly to prove to our kids, Oliver and Molly, that love can endure, to spare them the heartache of parents separating. I felt I had failed them and my future grandchildren.

For the last few years, I had tried to fix the subtle grumblings of his discontent, whilst at the same time coming to recognise mine. I felt that love conquered all, believed that marriage is worth fighting for. Both of us had experienced the loss and disempowerment of our parents divorcing, so I hung on with all my might for our children not to have the same fate.

The pain and grief of this earthquake ripping through my life was unbearable. After watching him leave, I realised life was presenting me with a choice — I could stay bound and stuck in anger and disappointment, or I could pick myself up, dust myself off, and choose love.

Up to this point, my beliefs and expectations were like fairy tales; romantic notions. I thought that my marriage would be lifelong, that all obstacles could be overcome, and that we would find a way to be besotted with each other again. Choosing love meant unbinding myself from old expectations of who I was and how I showed up in the world.

I learnt a new way of viewing love that involved healthier boundaries, self-empowerment, and compassion for myself. Choosing love was an invitation to live a truly Soul-led life, grounded in self-belief. Amidst the pain and grief of separation it was my lighthouse. A beacon of light, rising out of the darkness. A tall and stable safe harbour for my tumultuous sea of emotions.

Walking down this new, unexplored path guided by love was a process.

Although I did not know where the path would take me, it felt right. I felt completely supported and safe. Every turn offered me a friendly ear, a warm hug of encouragement and lucky synchronicities that propelled me forward, held my resolve and my focus, and encouraged me not to dwell.

Each step invited layers of me to be released. It was like I'd been wrapped up for years under many layers and, as I walked, I discarded one at a time, leaving a trail behind me. Each item discarded left me feeling lighter, freer, and more peaceful. Ultimately, I became comfortable in my own skin and accepting of my true nature, freckles and all. I know in my bones that I am lovable and that I have a beautiful love to give and share. I also knew I had to shed the layers that did not serve me.

The layers had kept me warm and cosy all these years, or so I'd thought. In fact, the warm fluffy scarf of not speaking up for my needs and wants had been strangling me. The heavy, waterproof coat had protected me from accessing my true feelings instead of allowing my tears to flow easily. The belt around my waist was a tourniquet for keeping 'everything together' even though it pinched.

Now I walk with a spring in my step, with my head held high. I feel light and free like a summer dress, blowing in the gentle breeze, unencumbered by expectations, and allowing my creativity full freedom of expression.

When the waves of emotion rise, I simply notice them, observe them, and let them take their natural course. Sometimes they crash to the shore, other times they gently ripple, caressing the sand. I am nurturing, compassionate and kind towards myself. I feel a wonderful sense of calm, with a constant subtle hum of loving support that is inside and outside of me all at once.

Life occasionally offers you the chance to contract, pause and expand once again. To bring you back into alignment with the truth of who you are. To love yourself and your life more than you dreamed possible, often when you least expect it.

Adapting to change can be a daunting prospect and yet I believe you are always supported and guided. That you are never given more than you can handle. And that if you allow yourself to be open and curious, life will show you the way.

You have within yourself all that you need to thrive. All the answers are within, truly they are. You are uniquely qualified to shine brightly as there is no other you. Being born with natural talents and the keys to unlock them is something you may not have been aware of until now. It's often the way; when you are naturally good at something, you may not be fully aware of it until someone, or something enlightens you or forces your hand.

The good news is that clues are everywhere and can be found in plain sight if you know what to look for. Sometimes they even literally fall into your lap.

Introduction

I didn't intentionally set out to write a book, it evolved through circumstance and serendipity.

I have always loved to write, to express my most intimate thoughts on paper. For as long as I can remember I have sought to understand myself and others, to appreciate how we 'tick'. I have an innate curiosity and drive to connect on a deep level with myself and others. And to be the best version of me that I can be.

When my 20-year marriage came to an abrupt and painful end, I needed an outlet. I reached for tools to soothe my broken heart and to make some sense out of my discombobulated thoughts and emotions. I began to journal, to pour out my thoughts, confusion and anguish onto the page. I noticed that on many days my writing had a poetic quality to it.

My journal entries evolved over time highlighting my healing and growth. A map or timeline from confusion to clarity, anguish to acceptance and self-deprecation to self-love developed in front of me. I found myself being able to articulate my feelings by writing them in story form. Going back to moments that stood out to me, that I could recall in visceral detail, aided my clarity and resolve. I also began to realise that my experiences may be of some benefit to others going through a similar ordeal.

I was a member of a writing group and so I shared some of my short musings and received some lovely feedback. I was told that my words touched people. Then came an opportunity to be part of a collaborative book around empowering women. I entered the competition with a 1500-word piece of writing about how I learned to live a life unbound. The words almost flew out of me and so I sent it off.

I was successful in becoming part of the collaborative book which ignited a spark within me. In a conversation shortly after the competition, my friend said: "Wow this could be an introduction to a book." That really got my cogs turning and the book project developed from there.

I collected my stories and journal entries together, tweaked and developed them with my story coach, and then added the tools I have learnt through a lifetime of self-enquiry that I felt would be supportive during times of unexpected change. The book was my sole focus for nearly a year; a way in and through my pain leading to clarity and contentment.

Guided by an ever-present intention to heal myself and to be of service to those whose lights had dimmed due to situations inducing self-doubt, a lack of self-worth and self-love, "Guided by Love" took form. A true labour of love. A project that gave me purpose and taught me so much.

This book is a gift of love from me to you. Within it you will discover some ways you disconnect from your true self and how to reconnect with yourself and others. I offer you some tools and exercises on how to keep in alignment with your own personal integrity, how to focus on and move forward with your life and feel a true sense of peace.

I will describe the nine key self-soothing tools to motivate positive thoughts and behaviours. You will discover your Nine Star Ki archetype and all its associated gifts. I will also tell you, how to work with the energy of your Nine Year Cycle to empower and enhance your life.

HOW TO USE THIS BOOK

There are moments in this book where I will invite you to participate.

Adults gain much more from practising the skills they have learnt and utilising ideas, than from reading alone. It would make my heart sing to know that this book has a positive influence on your life, that it has practical usefulness as well as offers support, comfort, and insights.

You can read the book from cover to cover, reading each chapter in turn; soaking up the stories, lessons, and healing.

You can intuitively flip to a page by asking a question, closing your eyes, flicking through the pages, and stopping when it feels right. Then study the guidance on the page you have chosen.

THERE ARE THREE DIRECTIONS IN THE BOOK:

- Take five Pause and Practice
- Take five Pause and Act
- Take five Pause and Journal

Take five Pause and Practice encourages you to practice a tool or exercise I have offered to enhance your experience, learning and growth.

Take five Pause and Act invites you to take an action such as playing a game.

Take five Pause and Journal invites you to take out a journal or notepad and give yourself some space and time to write down your unedited thoughts and feelings.

There are stories in the book where I share my experiences, some of which may be emotive for you. I felt it was important to dig deep into my emotions and share my truth intimately and candidly. I wrote this book for you as you may not have the words to describe your experience and yet they may be echoed through mine, bringing you insights, clarity and faith for a bright future.

I consider the journey I have been on a gift; I was set free because my Soul knew that I was abandoning myself in my marriage. I treasure the lessons I have learnt because I was able to create my life anew. A life where I can hear my truth and follow my heart's desires with confidence.

This is possible for you too.

Love and hugs

Lindsey x

PART 1
Cycles of Change

Chapter 1

CYCLES

You are influenced by and connected to many different cycles in life. From planetary and astronomical events - e.g., the moon which affects the tides, climate and weather, to biological - e.g., the menstruation cycle. Knowing that nothing lasts forever and is part of an ever-evolving cycle of change offers a light at the end of the tunnel. Even if life is tough right now, this too shall pass.

Following a seismic shift in your life, you can feel uncertain about who you are, what you have to offer, and what the future holds. Within this book I share how you can make good use of the cycles in your life. You'll learn how to move with the energy, not against it and to feel the power and freedom of recognising where you are placed.

You are a part of nature and are deeply intertwined and connected to her. Once you recognise her hidden codes and are familiar with how they are imprinted within you, she can open a whole new world to you. Nature has rhythms and predictable patterns which when viewed through certain lenses, give you a deep understanding of yourself. A view that enables you to shine brightly, design your life effectively and be in alignment with your true self.

I personally have been supported and guided by an ancient map based on cosmic cycles that has enabled me to make sense of who I am, where I am and where my strengths lie. I'm delighted that you now have access to this wisdom too. It's called Nine Star Ki and we'll delve into it shortly.

YOU HAVE A CHOICE

When my marriage ended abruptly, I made a choice to focus on love. To make choices and decisions from the heart and from love not fear. There were so many paths I could have gone down — anger, rage, bitterness — and yet I knew that only love would set me free. My training in Reiki, mindfulness and Nine Star Ki has taught me that your power is in the present moment. Change happens in the here and now. You have the power to choose who you are and what you stand for. To be so rooted in your truth that you will not allow it to be overridden by other people or circumstances.

That single choice enabled me to move through the devastation, grief and change without getting stuck. Instead, I experienced pauses and periods of time where I immersed myself in the feelings and thoughts that came up and allowed them to flow through me. To adapt, heal and grow.

I believe that cycles are a gift; opportunities to begin again in new empowered ways with the benefit of insight and growth. Some things are inevitable such as birth, death, the sun rising in the morning and the changing of the seasons. Life and the predictable natural passages of time do not wait; they march on whether we're ready or not, whether we want them to or not.

Choices are born from the awareness of new possibilities and perceptions. They can be intuitive, intellectual or learnt. They can be instantaneous or creep up on you over time. As the saying goes, it's easy when you know how. In the following chapters I will guide you through some insightful ways to make choices in life and relationships. To empower you and to support you.

Let's start with Nine Star Ki.

NINE STAR KI

I discovered many years ago, a map for life called Nine Star Ki. It shepherds you through the ever-changing energies and intricacies of life. It offers a blueprint for predictable patterns that show you how you are influenced by nature's cycles and how you can utilise this knowledge to gain greater levels of self-awareness and love.

Nine Star Ki (ki meaning energy) is the oldest form of knowledge about how energy moves through time. It is thought to be over 12,000 years old. Ancient peoples were very observant of their environment and intuitively understood that the astronomical cycles, seasons and climate influenced life on Earth, and planned their lives accordingly. From when and where they planted crops to which direction to build their homes in. They also noted that the timing of your birth has a great influence on your character.

YOU ARE MADE OF ENERGY

Everything in the Universe is made of energy including you. Energy has many names including *ki, chi*, Life-force, Spirit, Light, Aura and vibration or vibe. The name you know it by is not important — what matters is that you recognise it.

It's energy that gives you a zest for life, a sparkle in your eyes and the motivation to deal with tough things. When someone comes up behind you and you 'sense' them before they move or speak, you are sensing their energy.

You can feel the energy in a room when there has been an argument — the phrase 'you could cut the tension with a knife' comes to mind as the energy of anger is palpable. Equally the feeling of an awesome party where everyone is having fun can immediately lift your spirits and encourage you to join in.

YIN AND YANG

One of the main foundational principles of Nine Star Ki is the concept of yin and yang, the feminine and masculine forces of nature. These energies represent the opposites in nature which are needed for creation, movement and balance. The two energies of yin and yang meet in an everlasting dance, towards balance so there is never stillness, always movement. In practical terms, opposites offer insights and help us to discern. For example, knowing love is only possible when you experience the absence of it, feeling judged shows you how to be kind, feeling stressed can alert you to returning to calm and peace.

Day always fades into night. There are active times and times to simply be and receive. There are moments when things contract and expand again like relationships, the rhythm of your heart, and breathing.

Often when you feel like taking a certain action, the more effective approach is to do the opposite. For example, when you are feeling angry with someone and want to shout and scream at them. The more productive approach is to sit with the anger, to let it flow and take its course. Then respond instead of reacting. That way you have a much better chance of your needs and emotions being understood and met.

Equally instead of running away or hiding from an issue find the courage to face it and look it in the eyes until the fear dissipates. Dealing with it head-on enables you to reap the benefits. To recognise your strength and courage rather than allowing it to fester unresolved.

Sometimes when you notice that something is 'off' it may seem easier to shrug it off. In my experience, asking the person involved and giving them the opportunity to be honest is a courageous move. Being willing to ask a question that you may not like the answer to and staying open-hearted and open-minded to the answer is a true strength. It balances intuition (yin) with action (yang). Even if the other person does not reciprocate, you have done yourself proud. The truth always comes to light in the end.

MALE AND FEMALE ENERGY

John Gray in his book of the same name suggests that 'men are from Mars and women are from Venus'. The two energies of masculine and feminine are creative in different ways. Whilst you are healing, I'd encourage you to adopt the more feminine qualities of compassion, self-love and patience.

Whilst masculine energy tends to flow in straight lines, feminine energy moves in curves. Healing does not occur in straight lines; it is cyclical like a spiral curriculum. Masculine energy is best adopted when you need to take action.

Masculine energy is characterised by *doing* and achieving, and is shaped through logic and reason. In modern society it's the energy that is encouraged, favoured and even expected. The feminine is intuitive, oriented towards receiving and allowing, and characterised by *being*. This is the energy that society is learning to embrace now that it is clear; stress and overwhelm have a negative impact on productivity and well-being. When these energies are balanced, you experience a greater sense of harmony and fulfilment.

FIVE ELEMENT THEORY

The cyclic phases of yin and yang were developed into a theory called the Five Elements Theory by the Chinese Yellow Emperor in around 2600 BC. His deepening understanding of the energies of yin and yang motivated his writing of the classic work *Nei Ching*, the original book on Chinese Medicine.

Sometimes called the Five Transformations, it is a dynamic philosophy for understanding the living world. The five elements are wood, fire, earth, metal and water. The theory is that everything in the universe is an outcome of change, and results from the movement of the five elements and their relationship to each other.

Nine Star Ki uses the foundational energies of yin and yang, feminine and masculine and the five Elements, and divides them further into eight energies or phases positioned around a central point. The nine distinct energies are described by offering nine archetypes which will be explored in the coming chapters.

Knowing your personality archetype and remembering your strengths, especially in times of suffering, can be empowering and uplifting. It can help you overcome struggles by reminding you to dig deep into your gifts and skills.

PATTERNS

Nine Star Ki is a beautiful blueprint that offers a way of connecting with who you are on a deeper level. To help you discern which habits and patterns in your life would benefit from greater equilibrium.

I have found it to be an amazingly accurate, practical and insightful tool to guide me, since I discovered it around 11 years ago. It is a gentle, loving and encouraging wisdom that is profound in its simplicity. Nine Star Ki delights by unearthing hidden treasures and perspectives that were just under the surface waiting for you to find.

The system for determining your archetypal patterns is based on your date of birth. Nine Star Ki teaches that every year of your life has a specific plan and purpose. Being aware of where you are currently positioned in your personal time map enables you to navigate your activities, energy and emotions and get the best out of them, like working smarter not harder.

Nine Star Ki is a nine-stage cycle. It can be used as a nine-year cycle, and/or a nine-month cycle. Those are the main cycles, but there is also a daily cycle, an 81-year cycle, a 729-year-cycle and so on. Within the cycle are nine personality archetypes. There are patterns and symbolism imprinted within each of the nine stages, from 1: Water to 9: Fire that you can connect to for deep personal insights and valuable messages to guide you. The archetypes help you to gain a deep appreciation and love for yourself and others. Coming to know yourself, your talents, gifts and purpose as well as your emotional landscape, patterns and challenges offers valuable insights. It enables you to be more confident in all that you are and all that you do.

When you know who you are and what you stand for, it saves time and energy because you have a guideline to refer to. There is a theme for each year; a specific plan, meaning and purpose that brings focus to your life and offers detailed guidance for you to make the most progress each time. Each cycle has an emotional pattern associated with it that may influence your thoughts in unexpected ways. It is useful to be aware of these patterns ahead of time so that you can work with them instead of being confused or overwhelmed by them.

The more you can align with the energy of each stage of the cycle, the more easily life can flow. Each year is different to the year before and the year after, and so by understanding and immersing yourself in each year's theme, you are building and strengthening the foundations for future years too.

Each of the nine archetypes is steeped in symbolism from nature. Patterns and imagery including family dynamics help you to connect with and relate to the essence of each one.

You are not alone. There is a guiding, loving force in your life. You are connected to something bigger than you. There are purposeful invisible patterns in your life that, when followed, instil a sense of safety and reassurance. You have innate qualities and an energetic map to follow that can keep you from getting lost in the darkest times of change, loss and grief.

When you view life as presenting a loving force that is 'for you' and not 'against you', it will enable you to be braver, more creative and more secure in yourself.

Remember that feeling of everything being OK? The sense of calm, peaceful, assuredness that comes over you in moments when you feel loved, safe and secure? This book will show you how to capture that feeling every single day.

CHANGING ENERGY

Life is so much better when you have a good level of connection with the truth of who you are, and the flow of love that is all around you and available to you always. When you feel isolated or that you must face a situation alone with no support, everything seems harder, darker and scarier. With no outlet for your fear and stress, a vicious cycle can form. When you are alone with your thoughts, you can get immersed in stories that are not true and torture yourself unnecessarily. Easily getting fixated on perspectives that could be unkind, unloving and unhealthy.

When you connect to your true self, to other people and to the guidance around you, life takes on a vibrant buoyancy that you can track. You feel free to do what you want to do. There's no compulsion to check your phone or email every two minutes to find out what someone is doing or thinking. You can go ahead with your desired plans confidently without second-guessing yourself. You won't be so irritated or prickly with your loved ones and best of all know how to catch yourself when you feel stress rising.

They say change is as good as a rest. Although you may not be happy with the change you have endured, allow me to show you how reassuring it is to trust the process.

Chapter 2

CYCLE OF LOVE MAP

The Cycle of Love Map is intended to set the scene for the coming chapters. To give you context for how being guided by love works with Nine Star Ki and the practices contained within the book.

The fundamental premise of the model is:

Love is a process that involves action, expression and intimacy.
You are whole, perfect and loved.
Life's distractions can make you forget this.

There are tools and practices that remind you of the truth of who you are.

Love is a verb, it's an action word. Love is a process that requires expression, effort and application. It is a cyclical process that deepens with time and experience. Love is a process you can learn and build on to understand what you need to thrive in a relationship- with yourself and others. To journey through lust, infatuation and love, to find true love and true intimacy. The more you can move through the process consciously and intentionally the deeper the learning and greater the result.

On your journey through life so many things can veil the truth of who you are. Throughout this adventure called Life, remember please that you are loved beyond measure, that you have so much to offer the world by simply being yourself and that you are fundamentally OK. Through utilising the tools and practices within this book you will rediscover how loved, cherished and supported you are. How strong and courageous you can be and the inner resources you can draw upon when needed. You now have a toolbox to serve as a reminder of your awesomeness.

The Cycle of Love Map model offers six guidelines and is illustrated by a fruit tree. A tree represents strength. Just like you, they can stand tall. Trees grow up and outwards representing how a person grows stronger and increases their knowledge through experiences throughout their lifetime.

1. **Soil:** You are made of love; you go back to love, and in the middle (throughout your life), you can choose love. Love is your foundation. Just like soil, love provides nutrients, nurtures and supports.

2. **Roots:** You are born with a set of energies that are described through the Nine Star Ki which inform your personality/archetypes and influence what you do, say and think. Your roots also include family heritage and genetics.

3. **Trunk:** You have life experiences and are given certain messages from caregivers that form your beliefs and values. This forms your core, where you get your strength from. Recognising and observing unhealthy patterns in your family and deciding to heal them so they will end with you, is a powerful and courageous gift to all.

4. **Branches** are the extensions of how you live, how you reach out to people, and how you connect. Are you honest, brave and ask for what you want and need? Or do you shy away and avoid intimacy and connection? Has life taught you that you are amazing, encouraging you to reach for the sky and follow your dreams? Or are there areas of self-doubt and deprecation?

5. **Fruit:** What you harvest from those intentions, choices and actions. Is your fruit juicy and succulent or is it bitter? Is your life your mindset, home and work in alignment with your true self? Are you where you want to be? What comes out of you when you are squeezed, when you are stressed? Do you recognise it and choose self-compassion, or do you spurt out anger and frustration?

6. You can rise above instilled belief patterns and reach for the sky. Connect to the Universal energy of love. All you must do is choose it and then take guided action steps.

If you take a slice of a tree, you can see how it grew and under what conditions it lived in. You can also take an inventory of your life and look for how you have grown, what conditions you have lived in and how the conditions need to change for you to thrive.

TAKE FIVE PAUSE AND JOURNAL

Take a moment here to consider the following questions and write down your answers. Perhaps find a cosy corner, slip off your shoes and have a delicious drink to savour whilst you're here.

- What nurtures and nourishes you?

- Is it necessary to trim some branches, clear mental and physical clutter?

- What changes need to be made in your life to produce delicious fruit?

Life gives us opportunities to set intentions and make choices from either love or fear.

Love is an action

Love is a choice

It takes bravery and vulnerability to choose love and self-love, especially when you have experienced deep hurt. It is hugely rewarding to reach for the sky and to place yourself firmly rooted in the centre of your universe. To soak up everything that nurtures you first so that you can grow strong and then produce fruit that can provide sustenance to others.

Chapter 3

CYCLE OF CHANGE

A mentor once told me that we all have our own gifts and talents and that if we are interested in helping others, we can think about using those talents like being a driver on a bus route. Imagine you are a bus driver with one designated route, at each stop you pick people up and take them to their destination. Some people will stay a few stops with you, others just one or two.

Your route is just one aspect of the many journeys the passengers will embark on in their lives. Your role is to deliver them skilfully and safely from A–B depending on your specialist route. As your route is one of many for the people you encounter, you don't have to get bogged down in taking on the responsibility of getting them to another point on their overall journey.

I intuitively knew early on in my separation that I was navigating the twists and turns of this tumultuous life initiation in ways that would also be invaluable to you. Many people commented on how gracefully and lovingly I was working through the experience and one day it dawned on me that not everyone has the tools to do the same should they wish to. I understood that my marriage was a few stops along my route and was not destined to be part of my whole journey. But did others?

People began to ask me if I had always felt guided in some way, what the secret was to the way I chose to circumnavigate this heartbreak? They openly admired how I seemingly chose to pick myself up, dust myself off and concentrate on moving forward with my life unencumbered. That I chose love.

Reflecting on my journey from heartbreaking change to cultivating contentment, I was able to map out that path using the cycle of Nine Star Ki as a lens. I saw how I progressed through each stage of this cycle of change and what self-soothing remedies I adopted to heal and ride the wave. It wasn't a linear process as healing doesn't occur in straight lines. Like nature, healing is cyclical. For me it was a spiral, moving between the layers and coming back to thoughts and feelings to perceive them in more loving, empowered ways. Always building, each layer on the next.

There are so many experiences in life that can cause grief, shock and heartbreak. The death of a loved one, divorce, the ending of a friendship, the loss of a job. All come with a set of emotions such as anger, dejection and anxiety.

Exploring your thoughts and emotions is vital for healing. To move through them picking up wisdom along the way. You will oscillate between different stages of learning and healing as time goes on. The adage 'life goes on', whilst seemingly flippant when you are suffering, is true. Life goes on and change is certain. Having a blueprint or map for navigating a cycle of change enables you to heal consciously and intentionally.

Healing and recovery are absolutely possible after heartbreak and loss. It is important to appreciate though that there is no easy solution, no quick fix to moving through the pain. Fully expressing and processing your emotions is required for lasting change. The trigger cycle and your Nine Star Ki are really useful to refer to in moments of doubt and tumult to gain clarity, stop you getting stuck and to act appropriately.

THE TRIGGER CYCLE

The emotional centre of your brain (the amygdala) is designed to store sensory memory of your experiences throughout your life. When something is said or done (this could also be a facial expression or tone) that reminds your brain of a previous threatening experience, the old painful event gets 'poked' or reactivated — known as being triggered.

When you are triggered, you experience an intense physical, emotional and mental reaction. Being triggered can bring up flashes of memories, including images, feelings, and any sensory stimuli.

Triggers are healthy warning signs to help you question the situation, check in with yourself and determine what is okay for you. They are the signals you need to set boundaries and honour your needs, wants and values.

Your awareness around triggers — what causes them and how you react when they happen — is the most powerful way to start responding instead of reacting when feeling hurt or afraid. By figuring out ways to get that safety in the moment, without going through unnecessary reactions and conflict, saves a lot of time, energy, and heartache.

Whilst learning how to complete the cycle takes self-awareness, self-discipline, and lots of practice, the result will be safer and more connected relationships.

THERE ARE FOUR KEY PHASES OF THE TRIGGER CYCLE

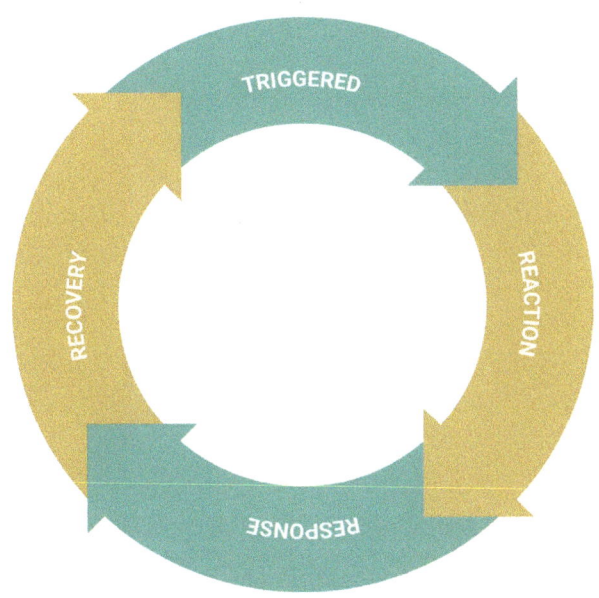

Triggered: A sudden intense emotional, physical, mental or spiritual reaction to a situation.

Reaction: Immediate outward reaction towards another person such as lashing out or withdrawing, coupled with an internal self-attack ('they don't care, I'm not worthy').

Response: Delayed response in an attempt to resolve the situation. Taking some time to rebalance. Expressing your needs and wants to the other person in a way they can understand and hear. Boundary communication.

Recovery: Feeling like the situation is resolved. Leading to rest, reflection, reset; finding wisdom and balance through the experience.

When the event — such as a breakup — is raw, you may get stuck between the reaction and response phases. This may look like self-blame and anger or resentment towards the other person. Your responses may oscillate between communicating healthy boundaries and frustration at not knowing how to express your needs.

Don't get despondent; remember it's all part of the cycle, the healing process. The important thing is to go full circle and complete the cycle so that you can recover.

The final stage of the trigger cycle is paramount to your entire healing journey. Recovery is the evidence that you can handle whatever life throws your way. You don't need to stay stuck between the trigger and the reaction phases, unable to find your voice for years. This is your opportunity to move through this experience, cultivating resilience and deepening your self-love with grace.

I was introduced to the trigger cycle by Samantha J Rix, Somatic Life Coach and Therapist and she beautifully describes this process as:

> *"Our emotional triggers are an opportunity to give love and compassion to the corners of ourselves that we haven't honoured yet!"*

I thank my lucky stars that I was able to move through the internal self-attack that sounded like: "What's wrong with me? I've failed! I just want to be loved for being me". Then learn how to recognise and move through my emotions like resentment (which stemmed from the sudden new status of single mum) by expressing my needs clearly no matter the outcome of my requests. Eventually to a place of balance, contentment and recovery. It took time. It required being really honest and facing some difficult truths. Plus sitting with uncomfortable feelings and working through loneliness and a longing for connection which I describe in coming chapters.

I know you can do it too. You've got this.

Chapter 4

NINE STAR KI: YOUR GUIDING STARS

When you were born the world was configured in a unique way. There was a specific energy in the atmosphere that you now carry as your constitution or archetype. On your birthday you were infused with the energy of the moment which shaped your personality, gifts, talents and the rhythm of your life.

Nine Star Ki is a map you can consult to help you heal, enhance self-awareness and plan so that you are in the flow of your life. It is like your love song to the world. When you know the tune, you can allow it to hum away to you in the background as a gentle guide and sing it loud and proud for all to hear and appreciate.

YOUR NINE STAR KI IS COMPRISED OF THREE NUMBERS; BIRTH, HEART AND SOUL.

First Number = Birth Star

Your optimal potential, your core energy; what drives you. To grow to your full potential often requires overcoming challenges and developing the strengths of this energy. This is your main energy that dances with the other two.

Second Number = Heart/ Inner Star

Represents where you go in times of stress and is the seat of your emotions. It's the wounded aspect of the inner child. Being driven by this energy is like being in the passenger seat of life. Healing these wounds can bring tremendous freedom and empowerment.

Third Number = Soul Star

This reflects how you do things in the world, how others often see you and indicates your hopes and aspirations. It is your Soul's highest evolution.

USING THE NINE STAR KI CHART

Before you dive in and use the chart to discover your archetypes there's a couple of things you need to know.

★Nine Star Ki is based on the solar calendar, a system built on the observed cycles of nature. Instead of a new year starting on 1st of January, it begins on 4th of February. This is because 4th of February is the mid- point between the solstice on 21st of December and the equinox on 21st of March. Over the centuries it was thought to be the most natural starting point for the year.

What this means for you is that if your birthday falls between 1st of January and 3rd of February, in Nine Star Ki you are considered as part of the previous year's group. For instance, if you were born on 1st of January 1980, in this system you use 1st of January 1979. Another example would be, if you were born on 3rd of February 2000, follow the 3rd of February 1999 Ki guidance.

When looking at the chart if you were born between 1st of January and 3rd of February, keep this in mind. It is only the year in these special circumstances that changes.

For any birthday between 4th of February and 31st of December, nothing changes and you do not need to do anything.

★Until you reach 18 years old or two cycles of nine, you are mainly living in and influenced by your inner or heart number. Once you reach adulthood then you will adopt your birth star energy. This may be a smooth transition or may take some getting used to as you navigate the new you and all the gifts and strengths it comes with.

HOW TO FIND YOUR BIRTH STAR

There is a method to find your birth star that involves a small amount of maths. This is useful for quickly working out someone's birth star, their main personality.

Truly understanding someone helps to make communication easier and build deeper connections. It's a gift to learn someone's love song to the world and sing it back to them.

This method works for any date in history.

Step 1

Add up all the digits of the year

e.g., 1981, 1+9+8+1=19

Step 2

Add these digits again if necessary until you reach a total of 10 or below

e.g., 1+9=10

Step 3

Once you have a number of 10 or below, subtract it from 11

e.g., 11-10=1

The Birth Star for 1981 is 1 Water

HOW TO FIND YOUR NINE STAR KI

Let's now discover your Nine Star Ki; the numbers are used as a shorthand to the elements.

1. Look at the chart below and find your year of birth. Then trace upwards until you find the corresponding birth star number between 9–1 which is a shorthand for your archetype.

For example:

If you were born in 1976 your birth number is 6

If you were born in 1980 your birth number is 2

If you were born in 1973 your birth number is 9

2. To find your full Nine Star Ki — all three numbers — locate your year of birth, then trace downwards and look to the left to find the row where the month and day of your birth fall. Your Nine Star Ki is the three numbers where your year of birth and day/ month of birth meet or intersect.

For example:

If you were born on 6th of March and your birth star is 4 then your 3 numbers are: 4.7.2

If you were born on 14th of May and your birth star is 7 then your 3 numbers are: 7.5.7

If you were born on 28th of January and your birth star is 1 then your 3 numbers are: 1.6.9

(Remembering that if you were born between 1st of January and 3rd of February, you have to go back one year.)

In Nine Star Ki all years begin on 4th of February and end on 3rd of February the following year, so any birthday between 1st of January and 3rd of February is considered to be in the previous year.

Examples: 14th of January 1977 changes to 14th of January 1976

3rd of February 1994 changes to 3rd of February 1993

4th February 1980 does not change because it's after 3rd of February.

NINE STAR KI CHART

9	8	7	6	5	4	3	2	1
1919	1920	1921	1922	1923	1924	1925	1926	1927
1928	1929	1930	1931	1932	1933	1934	1935	1936
1937	1938	1939	1940	1941	1942	1943	1944	1945
1946	1947	1948	1949	1950	1951	1952	1953	1954
1955	1956	1957	1958	1959	1960	1961	1962	1963
1964	1965	1966	1967	1968	1969	1970	1971	1972
1973	1974	1975	1976	1977	1978	1979	1980	1981
1982	1983	1984	1985	1986	1987	1988	1989	1990
1991	1992	1993	1994	1995	1996	1997	1998	1999
2000	2001	2002	2003	2004	2005	2006	2007	2008
2009	2010	2011	2012	2013	2014	2015	2016	2017
2018	2019	2020	2021	2022	2023	2024	2025	2026
2027	2028	2029	2030	2031	2032	2033	2034	2035

	9	8	7	6	5	4	3	2	1
4 Feb–5 Mar	9.5.9	8.2.2	7.8.4	6.5.6	5.2.8	4.8.1	3.5.3	2.2.5	1.8.7
6 Mar–Apr 5	9.4.1	8.1.3	7.7.5	6.4.7	5.1.9	4.7.2	3.4.4	2.1.6	1.7.8
6 April 6–5 May	9.3.2	8.9.4	7.6.6	6.3.8	5.9.1	4.6.3	3.3.5	2.9.7	1.6.9
6 May–5 June	9.2.3	8.8.5	7.5.7	6.2.9	5.8.2	4.5.4	3.2.6	2.8.8	1.5.1
6 June–7 July	9.1.4	8.7.6	7.4.8	6.1.1	5.7.3	4.4.5	3.1.7	2.7.9	1.4.2
8 July–7 Aug	9.9.5	8.6.7	7.3.9	6.9.2	5.6.4	4.3.6	3.9.8	2.6.1	1.3.3
8 Aug–7 Sept	9.8.6	8.5.8	7.2.1	6.8.3	5.5.5	4.2.7	3.8.9	2.5.2	1.2.4
8 Sept–8 Oct	9.7.7	8.4.9	7.1.2	6.7.4	5.4.6	4.1.8	3.7.1	2.4.3	1.1.5
9 Oct– 7 Nov	9.6.8	8.3.1	7.9.3	6.6.5	5.3.7	4.9.9	3.6.2	2.3.4	1.9.6
8 Nov– 7 Dec	9.5.9	8.2.2	7.8.4	6.5.6	5.2.8	4.8.1	3.5.3	2.2.5	1.8.7
8 Dec–5 Jan	9.4.1	8.1.3	7.7.5	6.4.7	5.1.9	4.7.2	3.4.4	2.1.6	1.7.8
6 Jan– 3 Feb	9.3.2	8.9.4	7.6.6	6.3.8	5.9.1	4.6.3	3.3.5	2.9.7	1.6.9

NINE STAR KI MAP

This map illustrates the cycle of change and shows where each of the nine archetypes sits in the mandala.

Mandalas are beautiful circular patterns that represent the Universe, completeness and self-unity. They can be used with inner reflection practices such as meditation which give you a sense of completeness and peace.

EXPERIENCE THE ENERGY

To get a good sense of your Guiding Stars let's take a tour, if you will, through the seasons in your mind's eye. You will likely recall that winter is very different to summer, and spring to autumn. That morning has a different energy from afternoon or evening. The seasons and cycles of time feel different, they have various qualities about them.

You hold all the elemental energies and qualities within you, however your guiding stars are more prominent. Your principal guiding star or archetype has the biggest influence on you. It will be evident in your life in all sorts of ways from the type of furniture you buy to the sorts of activities you enjoy doing.

A way to experience the cyclical nature of the seasons and the distinct archetypes within Nine Star Ki, is to take your attention to your breath and practice noticing the rhythmical, cyclical nature of breathing.

TAKE FIVE PAUSE AND PRACTICE

Take a moment to take a full breath, expanding your lungs. Experience the pause or transition from inhalation (breathing in) to exhalation (breathing out) and then exhale feeling your lungs and ribcage contract. Take some time to experience the sensations. Wait for the next inhalation to come by itself, no need to rush it.

Did you get a sense of everything rising as you took an inhalation? Your chest lifting upwards and your stomach expanding? Then that gentle pause, before your stomach started to slowly contract like letting air out of a balloon?

Inhalation, like the spring arrives, grows and builds until you get to the summer with that feeling of fullness at the end of the inhalation. And then as the breath goes out, experiencing that like autumn when things fall away, leaves fall; a contraction. And then at the end of the exhale, a quietness, stillness, a pause that is described as winter. Then out of that pause, springtime arrives and there is expansion through your lungs on the inhalation.

Breathing continues in the background without your attention.

The energy of your guiding stars behaves in the same way; it continues to support you in the background and now and then you will become mindful of its presence and will be able to seek and soak in its wisdom.

Each of the guiding stars in Nine Star Ki correspond to an element, season and time of day. To illustrate, here's a brief description of their characteristics.

WATER (1): NIGHT, WINTER

Water is the dark, quiet, potential and stillness of midnight and midwinter. It is reflection, prayer, meditation and sleep. People with this energy generally like to go with the flow, enjoy freedom, are intuitive and don't like too much structure.

WOOD/TREE (3,4): MORNING, SPRING

Wood energy is active like the beginning of a new day and the upward energetic movement of sunrise. It is filled with enthusiasm, creativity and new possibilities. People with this energy tend to be influential, driven and direct, although they are also vulnerable to self-doubt and anger.

FIRE (9): NOON, SUMMER

Like midday, Nine Fire is very active. It's the energy of peak summer where there's sunshine, parties and flowers in full bloom. It's the height of the midday sun as it illuminates our path. People with this energy are loving and passionate. Somewhat delicate and can wear their hearts on their sleeves.

EARTH (2,5,8): AFTERNOON, LATE SUMMER/ EARLY AUTUMN

Earth is the downward movement of the sun and the onset of autumn, also representing the transitional stage between the seasons of the year. People with Earth energy are nurturing, supportive and responsible. They give their resources freely and need to be sure to maintain good boundaries so that they are in service to others not servants.

METAL (6,7): EARLY EVENING, LATE AUTUMN

Metal is the inward, downward contracting movement of dusk and late autumn. Highly aware of details and have high expectations. Metal calls you to search for ways to refine your work and yourself. Metal people have an air of authority and are eager to help. Metal people can struggle with self-worth, they take their responsibilities very seriously.

THE NINE BIRTH STARS

Your Birth Star

Whilst the following descriptions are detailed and give you a huge insight, Nine Star Ki as a full modality is much more in-depth. I've been a student and a practitioner of Nine Star Ki for over a decade, and I cannot distil all its magic in a few chapters. If you would like to know more, I do offer individual personalised readings which go into your full Nine Star Ki (all three numbers) in detail, visit www.lindseyelms.com to connect with me and find out more.

1 WATER BIRTH STAR

Years:

1900, 1909, 1918, 1927, 1936, 1945, 1954, 1963, 1972, 1981, 1990, 1999, 2008, 2017, 2026, 2035

Imagery: Water, iceberg, waterfall, well

Time of day/ season: Midnight, winter, solstice

Family member: Middle son

The middle son (in the middle, between the other two sons) is diplomatic, helpful and independent. Always looking for a win-win situation in family life and arguments. Potentially very much at ease with all members of the family through using the skill of reflecting back everyone's feelings.

Signature strengths: Creative, innovative, easy-going, intuitive, diplomatic.

Catchphrase: Still waters run deep

Archetype

By observing and appreciating the qualities of water in nature, it is possible to connect with the qualities of the 1 Water personality.

1 Water energy is reflective, characteristic of contemplation, meditation and sleep. If 1 Water is your birth number, then your energy lends itself towards you being a deep thinker and from those depths come lots of ideas thus you have the capability of being an innovator. You take a philosophical view of life and are intuitive, sensitive and like to find meaning.

Water can be fresh, vital and active like mountain streams, appearing to be lively and positive with a spirit of adventure. At other times deep, brooding, slow and calm like ponds, lakes and the sea. You will display all 'colours' of the spectrum throughout your life at various times.

1 Water people have an independent nature which likes to explore. With the easy ability to find the way around obstacles in life, to see connections, and then consider objectively how to move them forward. Your ideas come from an inner knowing more than thinking.

1 Waters like to flow and enjoy freedom where possible and dislike being obstructed. You are not easily contained. You are therefore someone who values your own space and enjoys independence. With that space and depth, you have the opportunity to process emotions and experiences deep within you, this can sometimes take some time. If you tread water for too long, you may miss opportunities. Water also needs movement and flow otherwise it stagnates.

Like an iceberg, there can be lots going on beneath the surface with your emotions that others cannot see. The hidden part of yourself, the part that holds your emotions deep inside can be easily hurt as people may not recognise how you are feeling. Being a strong and often quiet person, you may not divulge how much you have been hurt and it may come as a surprise if you share it later. You can be stubborn and withhold information as you think other people do the same. Remember that communication is important and aids the integrity and quality of all your relationships.

Whilst you require lots of quiet time to be, your 1 Water energy also benefits from guidance and direction. Most water sources have some sort of container or structure to follow like a riverbank or a teacup. Without containment you can be chaotic and undisciplined — think of a river bursting its banks!

Guidance comes to you from your ancestors, intuition and the fabric of life. You are connected to everyone and everything, to the unknown and mysterious. Allow yourself to get still enough to hear the guidance available to you.

Famous 1 Waters

Captain Cook, Diane Keaton, Andy Warhol, Helen Mirren, Cameron Diaz, Bob Geldof, Chris Evert.

2 EARTH

Years: 1899, 1908, 1917, 1926, 1935, 1944, 1953, 1962, 1971, 1980, 1989, 1998, 2007, 2015, 2024, 2034

Imagery: The Earth

Time of day/ season: After lunch/ early afternoon in late summer

Family member: Mother

Mother energy is receptive, helpful, supportive, diplomatic and caring. The person you go to when you need a listening ear, a warm hug or something delicious to eat.

Signature strengths: Deep thinker, reflective, philosophical, intuitive, diplomatic.

Catchphrase: What can I get you to eat?

Archetype

2 Earth qualities are epitomised by the breastfeeding mother. The maternal energy that is caring, steady and reliable.

2 Earth energy is like lunchtime; a time for discussion. People with this energy are interested in other people's well-being and so will talk to others and ask questions to find out how they can be of assistance.

If 2 Earth is your birth number, you will naturally be good at finding out what's going on and what needs to be done. You are great at organising and are exceptionally kind and thoughtful. You will work away in the background to get things done. You'll be the one at the end of the party washing the plates and helping to tidy and clean up. You shine in a position of service although you are not a natural-born leader.

2 Earth energy is the quality of unconditional giving, symbolised by the Earth who gives you all her natural resources so that you can thrive. Family, friends and relationships are most important to you. 2 Earth folks are the peacemakers, incredibly loyal and patient.

Caregiving and mothering are a primal quality of life. In our modern-day society, this has been exploited and not honoured in the way it should be. Be aware of constantly giving your resources and carve out plenty of time for self-care. Give from the overfill of your cup rather than giving away your last drops of energy to other people. If you are stressed or unbalanced it can lead to feelings of martyrdom, resentment, being overlooked and a lack of boundaries.

You can find it difficult to receive so do watch out for overworking and being over-serious or compulsive. Do ask for what you need and want in a way that others understand clearly, i.e. be specific.

A frequent emotion for you is worried. This comes from the archetypal mother who wants to ensure her brood are all taken care of. This tendency does not serve you well as the worries tend to repeat and spin in your head. When you catch yourself worrying imagine yourself literally stepping out of the 'spin' to gain clarity and focus.

Famous 2 Earths

J.F. Kennedy, Marilyn Monroe, Michael Douglas, Daniel Radcliffe, Pablo Picasso, The Dalai Lama, Louise L. Hay.

3 Tree

Years: 1898, 1907, 1916, 1925, 1934, 1943, 1952, 1961, 1970, 1979, 1988, 1997, 2006, 2015, 2024, 2033

Time of day/ season: Dawn or sunrise / early spring

Imagery: Thunder, shoots breaking through concrete

Family member: Eldest son

The first-born son can explore, discover and try out things for the first time. An action taker and groundbreaker. Whether male or female, the eldest son is investigating what life has to offer for his future siblings.

Signature strengths: Action taker, optimistic, spontaneous, independent, visionary

Catchphrase: I'm getting on with it

Archetype

Imagine a new little shoot so excited and determined to be alive that it pushes its way through concrete. This is the energy of 3 Tree. As a 3 Tree, you are usually bursting full of ideas and creative expression.

3 Tree is the vital energy of early spring and early morning. Imagine sunrise, when the birds are singing, a new day full of possibilities is beginning and enthusiasm fills the air with a sense of childhood effervescence.

Your energy is impulsive and creative. It is an initiating, doing energy, that will likely have you bubbling with projects. Your drive is strong which can make you competitive. You have a warrior-like energy, strong, fierce and ready to act. You value doing over being.

Like the image of thousands of baby sea turtles clambering their way to the sea, or young shoots being squashed, not all your ideas will survive and come to fruition. You are fearless about trying new things and embracing your creativity. It doesn't matter if a creation doesn't work out, you fail fast and try again. If frustration turns to anger, you can be like thunder — boom, then it's out of your system and over!

3 Tree energy is quite vulnerable, especially when the spirit of effervescence is oppressed. Life has a way of stifling you at times. When you have a plan, you like to action it and if it doesn't materialise or go efficiently it can be incredibly frustrating for you. Whilst you value your independence it's OK now and then to seek the support of others.

In conversations you tend to like directness and don't enjoy long discussions about a problem. You want to cut to the chase, figure out what's wrong then fix it. You can enjoy challenging others in interactions turning conversations into debates that you like to win. Be mindful that this style of interaction can be perceived as pushy or aggressive which may need to be softened with other personalities.

Sometimes 3 Tree energy can lead to self-stagnation through overthinking or mentally generated stalemate. The antidote to this is to physically move: dance, play a sport, go for a run.

Famous 3 Trees

Barack Obama, Robin Williams, Charlie Chaplin, Vincent van Gough, Frank Bruno, Gabrielle Bernstein, Kyle Gray.

4 Tree

Years: 1897, 1906, 1915, 1924, 1933, 1942, 1951, 1960, 1969, 1978, 1987, 1996, 2005, 2014, 2023, 2032

Imagery: The wind, trees, bamboo

Time of day/ season: Late spring and late morning

Family member: Eldest daughter

The first-born daughter is always searching for new ways to express her creativity and work. Typically expected to look after the parents in older age, she may sometimes feel a sense of disappointment, like she has missed out on all that life has to offer. She can give guidance and inspiration to her younger sisters.

Signature strengths: Tender, adaptable, practical, thoughtful, reliable, great common sense, conversation

Catchphrase: I'm not sure about that

Archetype

4 Tree energy is like a gentle wind; easy-going, gentle and open-minded. Like the wind you can be very adaptable and resourceful, changing directions as needed. If you allow yourself to bend like bamboo and be flexible, you can be an ingenious creator. You have a great capacity for vision and can be ahead of the times. However, you don't tend to plan too far ahead, preferring to take things step by step and enjoy surrendering to the present moment.

You have a charming approach to life and are incredibly tender and kind. To others you may appear to be lucky, this comes from being in the flow of life. When you are fully connected and available to grace, things naturally come to you. 4 Tree energy can be beautifully utilised as the 'wind at someone's back' supporting and gently guiding. This energy lends itself well to coaching, mentoring, counselling and being a good friend.

Be cautious not to overanalyse, overthink, stagnate or give in to self-doubt as adaptability out of balance can lead to overwhelm and procrastination.

Fear of judgment can make it difficult for you to ask for help and be over-guarding of your feelings — remember people love to help and support you so do reach out. Friends will be only too happy to help and will not think you are complaining! Don't isolate yourself. If you need an outlet, talk to someone.

You like to feel in charge and in your power and so when others shame, belittle or cut you down, you hate it. This treatment can make you feel small, silenced and dimmed. Remedy this by accepting that not everyone thinks or perceives things in the same way and love your individual uniqueness.

Just like plants break through the soil, 4 Tree people are the ones who create breakthroughs in old, outdated ways of being. You have a natural creative drive that needs to be directed into something positive — a task or cause that can benefit humankind, otherwise you can get restless.

You are likely to challenge the status quo or question unnecessary rules, and will use your creativity to find alternative routes and solutions. If your progress is blocked, then your emotional response is anger. This can look like being too hard on yourself although you'll be more upset if you think someone else is putting obstacles in your way. The negative version of anger is destruction. The healthy version is drive — use anger like a booster rocket!

Famous 4 Trees

William Shakespeare, Galileo, Albert Einstein, Martin Scorsese, Usher, James Corden, Nicole Scherzinger, Katie Holmes.

5 Earth

Years: 1896, 1905, 1914, 1923, 1932, 1941, 1950, 1959, 1968, 1977, 1986, 1995, 2004, 2013, 2022, 2031

Imagery: The central point, a wheel, an earthen bowl, the ying yang symbol

Time of day/ season: The pause between seasons

Family member

Part of the family and yet relatively distant from the other members. Takes on the qualities of all the other eight stars.

Signature strengths: Leadership, guidance, catalyst for healing and change, bold, great at systems/ analytical

Catchphrase: What's the strategy?

Archetype

5 Earth is the centre: a catalyst, all energies touch it and it touches all other energies. It is a very strong supportive energy. Think of being 'centred' or having a reference point or place to come back to when life's challenges and emotions pull you off balance. The centre is the place you know you have to come back to.

If you are a 5 Earth, then you are a powerful force of nature. An image of this energy is a wheel. It is the hub, like in the centre of a turning wheel, people often look to you for leadership and guidance. You can help 'turn things around' for them. You are resilient, resourceful and a natural problem solver. 5 Earth people have a very stabilising energy and tend to be practical, organised and have lots of common sense. With extraordinary problem-solving abilities, you can come up with solutions for individuals and groups making order out of chaos.

Being outside the 'family', gives you a tendency to learn from your own difficulties and experiences. Sometimes situations can be extreme, involving success and failure. You can bounce back from life's ups and downs and have great resilience.

Like a toddler experiencing the world, you wander round like a mini sumo wrestler, wide-eyed, curious and determined. The strength in a toddler's belly and gait makes them resilient and centred. They will not be held back in their explorations and will bounce back from discoveries that were painful or frightening.

5 Earth is a powerful and grounded energy. Your heart knows how to ground and centre you so that you can be a catalyst to move through challenges. Your presence is likely to stir change in others. You may notice that at times people around you are not ready to receive your natural 'stirring' quality, you will know by their response to you. Your presence can create an intensity. This is wonderful when people light up with new ideas and are well received (usually they won't know why, they'll just have a sense that being around you facilitates awareness). It can be disarmingly uncomfortable if they are not willing to change in some way and so unfortunately you may find yourself at the sharp end of the stick.

You are often in the centre of things and people are naturally drawn to you. Community and connection are very important to you. Seek out people who recognise and welcome your energy, that welcome your insights. Spend less time with people who drain you or do not raise you up.

You are at your most contented and balanced when you are being of help to others and being recognised for your efforts and achievements. You are endlessly caring and will show up as a strong support for others. You are the solid ground beneath our feet and a source of healing and nourishment.

A lack of acknowledgement for your contributions coupled with movement from all angles can make you unsure of your place in the world and can lead to self-doubt. Thus, you have a strong longing to find a place or a niche for yourself. Be sure to use your gifts for yourself too as a lack of self-care and awareness can make you complain, be impatient and blunt. Remember that no matter what else is going on around you that you are loved, and you are the most important person in your life.

Famous 5 Earths

Mahatma Gandhi, Sir Walter Raleigh, Henri Matisse, Richard Attenborough, Usain Bolt, Millie Bobby Brown.

6 Metal

Years: 1895, 1904, 1913, 1922, 1931, 1940, 1949, 1958, 1967, 1976, 1985, 1994, 2003, 2012, 2021, 2030

Imagery: Father, Heaven, sword

Time of day/ season: Evening in late autumn

Family member: Father

A father takes responsibility for the family and are known for their fair dealing of situations. Whether you are a male or female 6 Metal, you will come across as straightforward with a natural air of authority. Sometimes the wish for fairness and rationality can appear too rigid.

Signature strengths: Natural leader, authority, loyal, moral, direct, noble, rational, wise

Catchphrase: What is the truth here?

Archetype

Metal is associated with autumn — the leaves are turning red and yellow and are falling off the trees, the weather is becoming crisper, and the daylight becomes shorter. All around there is a process of letting go, exhaling and eliminating what is no longer needed, making space to inhale inspiration.

6 Metal carries a powerful energy, symbolised by the divine father. Father energy is loving and respectful and as such people listen to you. There is no 'if', 'but' or 'maybe' with this archetype. You tend to think that you are right and especially about what others need to do. This energy is sharp and focused like a horse with blinders on.

You are a natural leader and have a strong sense of justice. You prefer to give advice, rather than take it. 6 Metal is a protective energy that can be strong, authoritative, precise and practical. Family is very important to you, and you are the most loyal of all the archetypes. You use your wisdom and wit like the edge of a sword to cut through the extraneous and get to the heart of the matter. Accuracy activated by wisdom and tenderness.

You have a creative energy that enables you to initiate/ activate projects and then complete them with precision and discernment. With a capacity to focus you get things done!

Clarity comes down from the energy of 'heaven' into your crown which shows up as a strong intuition. Metal has the ability to accrue wisdom and make decisions and refinements. This energy brings everything together in a melting pot and alchemises it into gold, impurities being cast away.

Any process where you are seeking answers or higher knowledge is a very metal activity. In the forefront of your mind are big questions like 'What is life all about?' With the ability to access deep equanimity, to be quiet and centred at your core and embodying the power of divine light, expressed through the heart you can use your intuitive gifts to serve others in a beautiful way.

The ability to be calm and clear can be overlooked by yourself and others due to society's tendency to encourage doing, doing, doing. The prevalence of 'just keep doing' enables the voice in your head to frequently suggest that you are not good enough which drives you to do more, often leading to self-criticism. Think of a stereotypical family father and his need to provide. Holding this energy expresses as a tendency to feel a tremendous sense of duty and responsibility.

Now that you have an awareness of this tendency, you can recognise it and use your sword to prune what no longer serves you such as harsh, critical and cutting self-talk and replace it with a warmth and sweetness to soften that edge.

Famous 6 Metals

William Wordsworth, Captain Scott, Desmond Tutu, Madonna, Wayne Dyer, Justin Bieber, Reece Witherspoon.

7 Metal

Years: 1894, 1903, 1912, 1921, 1930, 1939, 1948, 1957, 1966, 1975, 1984, 1993, 2002, 2011, 2020, 2029

Imagery: A still lake, jewellery

Time of day/ season: Evening in autumn

Family member: Youngest daughter

The youngest daughter brings all the experience that coming into the family last can provide. A carefree spirit arising from the secure knowledge other more responsible older siblings will take care of the details and worry. A reflective quality shines through with a youngest daughter, in spiritual, emotional as well as in amusing ways.

Signature strengths: Fun loving, outgoing, receptive, good listener, charismatic and graceful

Catchphrase: Isn't that beautiful?

Archetype

If your birth number is 7 Metal, you are in tune with the lighter side of life. You are all about fun, being sociable and relaxation. Your days are filled with accomplishing beautiful things with grace. Your energy is associated with sunset, autumn and reaping the rewards of the harvest. A time of accomplishment and the joy of success whilst celebrating with friends and family.

7 Metal energy is focused on achieving beauty, people with this energy see beauty in all things and they inspire us. You have a wonderful touch in art and music/sound, and exhibit an instinctive sense of how to make a space gorgeous.

You like things to look good including yourself, and so you are likely to have a wardrobe filled with lovely clothes. You take care of yourself physically by exercising and having self-care treatments such as massages or facials.

Like the element of metal, you are very good at reflecting the qualities of the environment and telling others what they need to hear, this is symbolised by the lake. You notice the energy around you, the vibes and essence of what people say and don't say. Rather than sharing your observations openly you will often take what you have learnt and decide how you can best utilise it for yourself. For example, if you notice a parent behaving badly, you won't necessarily call them out, instead you will vow not to behave in such a way yourself as you have recognised the unhealthy pattern.

It can take you quite a bit of time to reveal how you truly feel as you are deeply private. You tend to worry about being good enough and can be overanalytical and perfectionistic. Your focused energy can be stubborn at times, and you can go into denial, trying to keep the surface of that lake smooth and perfect. As you are so good at reading others, you require space and alone time, a chance just to be yourself. People close to you will need to recognise the signs of brooding and gently nudge you to open up and express your emotions.

When you have a good balance of inner and outer reflection time, you can be charming, quick-witted and make a great host. You have a flair for communication and expressing yourself. You can make people smile and laugh which is a good talent to have.

Famous 7 Metals

Sir Isaac Newton, Sean Connery, Scarlett Johansson, David Beckham, Katie Winslet, Angelina Jolie, will.i.am.

8 Earth

Years: 1893, 1902, 1911, 1920, 1929, 1938, 1947, 1956, 1965, 1974, 1983, 1992 2001, 2010, 2019, 2028

Symbolism: Mountain with a cave

Family member: Youngest Son

The youngest son has had the benefit of observing and taking onboard everybody else's dramas and triumphs. He has had the opportunity for reflection and is therefore very good at expressing the accumulation of knowledge, particularly in an intellectual way.

Signature strengths: Strong, stable, persistent, composed, contemplation, strong sense of justice and fairness.

Catchphrase: Is this fair?

Archetype

8 Earth is the time between deep winter and spring when the seeds underground are coming alive. The seeds of change are within you and as such you have a revolutionary energy. You use this strength to support change. In nature the image for 8 Earth is the mountain. Mountains are strong, immovable and you can lean on them. Mountains also tend to support all sorts of life on their slopes. 8 Earth people take their responsibilities very seriously. They are hardworking, reliable and steadfast in the face of difficulty.

By holding the strength of a mountain, life will give you opportunities to use this gift, so that you can recognise it. Therefore, you can take on or are handed difficult challenges and responsibilities in life. You did not come to coast, you came to transform like a butterfly. Your primary energy is the ultimate space holder for the transformation and evolution of your own and other people's lives. You have a deep nurturing quality and will go to great lengths to support others, often when no one else will.

Taking the analogy of the mountain further, you are firmly planted in the Earth and so do not move quickly. You tend to move through life methodically, intentionally and with purpose. You have a slow and meticulous attention to detail which you can get lost in and can frustrate some! It can sometimes seem that nothing is being done, however your action deepens rather than spreads — you delve down into what you want to pursue.

Getting too bogged down in the details instead of reviewing the big picture can result in feelings of confusion and not being able to prioritise. The remedy to that is reaching out to others for encouragement and suggested ways to take action so you can get your feet back on the ground.

Within the mountain is a cave. As your emotions are linked with mountain energy, it is important that you spend time in your cave in silence and contemplation to receive wisdom and listen to your innermost thoughts and guidance. A cave could be your car, a den, or a space in your house that's quiet where you can be alone when needed. Without this time, you can become stubborn and uncommunicative, and a caller at your cave could get a surprise with the sharp end of your tongue. In a clear and grounded state, you are skilled at using your accumulated knowledge and sharing it i.e., teaching others to discover their own buried treasure.

Famous 8 Earths

Beatrix Potter, Arnold Schwarzenegger, Elton John, Stephen Spielberg, Chris Hemsworth, Amy Winehouse, J.K. Rowling.

9 Fire

Years: 1892, 1901, 1910, 1919, 1928, 1937, 1946, 1955, 1964, 1973, 1982, 1991, 2000, 2009, 2018, 2027

Symbolism: Fire (from a flame to a forest fire), the heart

Family member: Middle daughter

Streetwise, expressive and sparky, when you meet a 9 Fire you will not forget them easily. The middle daughter can shed light quickly on the problem at hand, with a laser focus she will come to conclusions and help those around her see what is obvious. This challenging and direct nature can be dazzling.

Signature strengths: Inspiring, outgoing, passionate, warm, strong, heart-centred, expressive, active.

Catchphrase: Let's spread some love

Archetype

9 Fire is the energy of midsummer and noon, a peak time for activity. A vibrant, active energy that encompasses all the qualities of the sun. It is bright, rapid expansion and full speed ahead.

9 Fire people are full of passion, charismatic and social. They burn brightly and are usually easily noticed, although some may be quieter. They are open-hearted, outgoing and thoughtful. They express and spread love and joy. They are affectionate and have a sweetness about them.

If you are a 9 Fire you can burn brightly for all to see when you express yourself fully. With a highly creative mind, activity and variety are important to you. You are a quick learner and have a constant drive for accomplishment and fulfilment. Acknowledgement from others can motivate you so be sure to say so if you need 'stoking'.

You lift people's spirits up, are charming and fun. You are gifted with making others feel happy and inspired. The phrase "Oh that looks like fun" will be a regular part of your vocabulary!

You are a busy person who generally has lots of balls in the air. You can manage your projects effectively by working on them in short bursts. Fire drops away to ash and goes still as part of its process so a healthy 9 Fire will schedule rest to be balanced and content.

Cultivating your relationship with Fire will assist you to become more self-aware and utilise your strengths. Some questions that you can ask yourself as a 'check-in' are:

- Do I need the energy of home fires (heart, passion, compassion)?
- Do I need the focus of a candle flame?
- Am I being catastrophic in my thinking?

Out of balance you can tend towards catastrophic thinking and/or chaotic behaviour. You may lash out or think: 'It's all gone to hell'. When you witness this within yourself bring it back and contain it by paring back your activities. Think of this pattern as a forest fire that started as a spark and then spread out of control.

Nines also tend to have a vulnerable heart, and you may easily find yourself being emotional around someone who is upset. This is because you are an empath and so easily relate to and feel the anguish of other people. Be mindful of your own energetic boundaries and ensure that you are not absorbing too much of other people's energy mistaking it for your own. Remember that not every thought or feeling is yours when you are in close proximity or thinking about someone else.

Whilst it's lovely to be supportive of others, it is very draining on your energy to process emotions that aren't yours.

Due to your vulnerable heart if you experience betrayal, hurt or loss please don't allow it to close your heart. Your strength is to spread love, to offer affection and connection. If you close down not to feel pain, you will also close off your capacity for joy and happiness too.

Famous Nine Fires

Jane Austen, Walt Disney, Martin Luther King, David Bowie, Kate Moss, J.R.R. Tolkien, Paula Radcliffe.

HOW NINE STAR KI HELPED MY HEALING JOURNEY

Since I discovered it, Nine Star Ki has helped me to be present and mindful of my thoughts and actions. This spiritual practice was incredibly helpful during my heartbreak journey and continues to support me now. It enabled me to understand myself better and where I was situated in my personal time-map which acted like a guiding light during my darkest days.

Knowing my Nine Star Ki pattern, which is 4.1.8, and choosing to use it as a measure against my responses enabled me to be less reactive and overwhelmed. It was a handy reminder that I am driven, adaptable and gentle, yet prone to self-doubt. That I am a helpful person; a deep thinker who always looks for a win-win in a situation and yet prone to being consumed by fear. And that I am strong and nurturing yet pre-dispositioned towards stubbornness.

Being aware of my strengths enabled me to tap into them, to turn them up like using an equaliser to manage my emotions on particularly hard days. Recognising when I was slipping into the challenging aspects of my personality helped me to take a step back rather than being overcome and governed by my heightened emotions.

My 4 Tree energy has helped me to be flexible in my thinking, to consider other people's perspectives, to be kind to myself and to focus on a way into and through my pain. I was able to recognise when I was holding onto disappointment and the negative impact that had on my ability to let go. To notice when I acted as the 'wind at someone's back' far longer than was healthy for me and to stop and take care of myself instead.

My 1 Water energy has aided me to 'go with the flow' of life, to recognise that there will always be obstacles and to avoid stagnating by finding ways to float downstream. Trying to fight against the current is fruitless and tiring! 1 Water energy helped me to dive deep into the source of my thoughts and feelings so I could emerge back up on the surface with fresh perspectives. There were also times when my intuition whispered to me (even shouted; loudly), and I resisted the truth until I dared to accept the necessity for change.

My 8 Earth energy enables me to be self-reflective, accumulate knowledge and have the strength of a mountain. To nurture myself and those around me. There were times though when I was resistant to reaching out to others for support, feeling that I 'should' show my best face and not let anyone know the pain I was in, to hide it deep inside the mountain cave. I got stuck and bogged down instead of looking out from the mountaintop to see the bigger picture.

My break-up also occurred at the beginning of a new Nine Star Ki year, a 4 year in my nine-year cycle. The fact that it happened then suggested to me that this life-changing shift was to become the central focus of the year. The Nine Star Ki years will be further explained a little later in the book. But for now, to give you some context, a 4 Year is all about change and rapid growth followed by a 5 Year which is all about healing.

Knowing that I was immersed in the energy of change allowed me to gradually soften into acceptance. Life was letting me know that it was time, it was meant to be. That the energies of my personal time map had aligned for my rapid growth of which my marriage was a casualty. It was comforting to be aware and that the following year would offer healing and the years after reaping the benefits of change and growth and finding joy. This knowledge gave me some peace and something to hold onto and focus on.

TAKE FIVE PAUSE AND PRACTICE

Now that you know what your Birth Star's natural strengths and qualities are, I invite you to reflect on where and when you notice these patterns appearing in your daily life. Intend to notice how the energy guides your movements, behaviours and feelings. Sometimes the energy can be subtle like a soft breeze and other times you will recognise it with the clarity of a lightning rod.

Chapter 5

MAYA'S STORY

Maya

As the logistics of the seismic change ahead of me started to bombard my head, thoughts spun round like a spinning top and every now and then a clear question would pop out: What about the dogs?

It felt like time was of the essence because he was packing up to go, so I thundered quickly downstairs and found him sorting clothes out in the den. Molly had caught up with me and we stood in the doorway between the kitchen and den. I asked in a direct yet slightly panicked tone: "What about Maya? What about the dogs? Do you want me to look after them?"

Maya was his dog, a gift from me several years before. After he had been on a trip with friends and their Patterdale, he had waxed lyrical about them. I was driving along a lovely country road not long after the trip and a thought popped into my head: "Wouldn't it be great to get him a Patterdale puppy?" I was initially surprised by that out-of-the-blue thought, however as I drove along, a feeling of excitement started to rise within me. Anticipation began to bubble up from my tummy to my heart, a warm fizzy sensation that erupted into all sorts of thoughts and plans.

"It's doable", my mind suggested with a smile arriving on my face. "Yes, it is a good time. I am working part-time now so there would be someone around, and the puppy would get plenty of attention and not be left alone for long periods. We could go for more walks as a family, and he would be over the moon." I imagined seeing my husband's delighted face and that filled me with joy. I loved to see him happy, and the bonus would be all the benefits to the whole family.

I hatched a plan to get a puppy for his birthday later that year. I trawled the internet for advice and information on the breed and where to look for a reputable breeder. I even did all the research covertly on my phone using a different search engine to the one on our shared computer. I had discovered not long before, by way of a playful comment, "Ah I know what you've been doing today" that he could easily see what I had been looking at on our home computer. I felt so proud of myself for creating such a special surprise for him.

I found a breeder I was happy with and so the day came to meet the puppies for the first time. I was thrilled that we were the first people to meet them so would have the whole litter to choose from. The breeder had asked if we would want a boy or girl, tan or black and so I let him know it was a surprise and entirely my husband's choice.

I took him over to the breeder's house on the pretence that we were picking up a washing machine for my mum. I could barely contain my excitement and I thought he would surely suss that something was amiss as I couldn't hide it! As the breeder opened the front door and we heard the dogs barking, I turned to him and said: "We're not really here for Mum, we're here for you. Go through and choose one." With a slightly confused look on his face, he went inside the house. Once he saw the puppies and realised what was going on, he looked over at me and said: "Really?" with a big smile on his face.

He focused on Maya straight away; it was love at first sight. He went straight to her and picked her up gently. "Hello you" he said with a sparkle in his eye, and I knew instantly that she would be the one we would take home.

Now standing in the doorway, he looked up at us and said: "I'm not taking her with me, she can just be rehomed."

Molly and I stared at him in utter disbelief. And then we both screamed at him.

Molly said clearly shaken and very upset: "You can't say that she is meant to be your dog, how can you say that?"

She couldn't believe what she was hearing, what her dad was saying. Later she told me how much that moment had upset her and how confusing it was. She felt like he was being heartless and was so angry with him that she wanted to punch him.

I was shocked, disbelieving and enraged when those words came out of his mouth. Perhaps said in the heat of the moment whilst trying to escape from our questions, and yet he had uttered them. My head couldn't wrap around the idea that he could so easily abandon, potentially give away, a beautiful being that he apparently loved. I was furious that he could even think that way.

I understand now that part of my anger was fear. Fear that if he could treat his beloved dog that way then it wasn't too much of a stretch to give the same treatment to myself and the kids. To abandon us. To throw us away.

Maya stayed with us of course, along with her beautiful son Pepper. She laid on the bottom stair next to the front door for weeks, regularly looking out of the window for her dad to come back. She barely ate and was very subdued. When I looked into her eyes, I could see how sad and dejected she felt. Pepper was clingy and needed a lot more reassurance, and since then he has been very sensitive to raised voices. They were both as heartbroken as we were.

PART 2

Go within & Discover

Chapter 6

CONTRACTION

One of the most profound ways to understand yourself at your core is to experience a contraction in life. An experience that rocks your foundations and perceptions so much that you have no choice but to surrender to the change. To open your mind and heart to the lessons life is offering to you. To surrender and fall back into the supportive arms of the love around you and inside you.

Contractions in life tend to be painful, excruciating even at times, and can make you feel small and demoralised. You can feel like the wind has been taken out of your sails and you are stranded out to sea without hope of rescue. However, just like contractions in labour, the ultimate prize is new life. The hardest part of birth is towards the end, just before the baby arrives when women often feel like they can't go on; that they have hit a wall. It's common for women to say they can't do it; they have run out of energy and the pain is too much. Yet moments later when they are holding their baby in their arms, there is a rush of love and pride. The pain all worth it and the memory of the birth all but forgotten.

I remember as clear as day the joy and pride I had when my children were placed on my chest after giving birth. Looking down at them with awe and love. Mesmerised at the perfect beings I had the privilege of growing and bringing into the world, I felt so amazed at what I was able to create.

Contractions always lead to expansion. Pausing to learn what they are teaching you is a beautiful gift to self and will ripple out to everyone around you.

DISCONNECTION

Disconnection is extremely painful, especially when you have been deeply connected to someone or something and it is taken away. It can feel like a dark, lonely and isolated place, with little light at the end of the tunnel.

When I first felt the pain of disconnection, the enormity of what it meant to be separated landed with full force in my mind and body like a blunt trauma from a sledgehammer. I reeled under the realisation that I was no longer part of us. My mind went into overdrive, into complete panic. It was flooded with thoughts of "What am I going to do?" and "What if?".

It felt unbearable. I didn't know what to do with myself, I wanted to run away, escape; for it all to be a bad dream. I remember lying on my sofa, my heart pounding so hard and rapidly it felt like it would come out of my chest. It had never thumped so violently before, and it scared me.

"You'll be OK," a friendly, calm voice echoed in my head. "You're having a panic attack, the worst thing that will happen is you will faint and wake up again. Just lay down and breathe."

My body was telling me in no uncertain terms how panicked she was. Then, worried that the kids may be distressed at seeing me like this, I pulled a blanket up close to my face and snuggled it. Pleading with my body and mind to relax.

I placed one hand on top of the other over my panic-stricken, thumping, broken heart and took some deep breaths. The warmth of my hands felt soothing and nurturing and, whilst breathing deeply and gently, I finally dropped off to sleep.

Disconnection is painful because there is a sense that something is missing, that something has been lost. With that comes a sense of yearning and grief. When feeling disconnected often the smallest of actions to further cut ties can cause distress, emotional and physical pain and anguish. Particularly in relationships where you were connected by so many threads that held meaning and memories. When they are severed it can feel like a piece of your heart has been ripped out.

I remember the pain and grief of realising that I would never again experience things that were specific to us that I had grown so accustomed to. Our 'us' was gone. I would have to cook all my own meals, drive myself and the kids everywhere we needed to go, and take the dogs for a walk without the catch-ups or the male voice of authority that they responded to.

Ultimately it was the loss of my family unit that was the hardest to bear. The romantic notion of walking down the street holding hands when we were old and wrinkly vanished, along with sharing the joy of our future grandchildren; and the wider family parties would no longer be possible, or at least in the same way.

I had to let myself feel the pain of each layer of disconnection and all that went with it such as feeling disappointed, sad and trapped. The emotions came in waves over time, not all at once; with each layer came more acceptance, space and peace.

It took me a while to realise that, through wanting so badly to save my marriage, I had taken my attention and focus completely away from myself. I searched for ways to fix, repair and prove. I bought book after book around relationships, listened to podcasts, soaked up short courses and yet nothing helped. In fact, the space between us got bigger and bigger. The more I tried, the more I was met with silence and resistance.

Although I had learned a lot about relationships and how to cultivate more love, intimacy and connection, these months had shown me all the ways they were missing. Eventually I was able to throw away my rose-tinted glasses.

I realised how important emotional connection was to me. I discovered that no matter how much we are bonded to others, it is vitally important that connection to ourselves is nurtured first and foremost. It was like a light was turned on in my head, having been in a dark room searching for the switch. I could see clearly the necessity to pause and explore who I was and wanted to be — my values, needs and non-negotiables — before I moved forward.

There are patterns that you can fall into when feeling disconnected, harbouring in the hope that they may serve as a remedy to reconnect. Unfortunately, these ways of attempting to close the gap can often make the space cavernous instead.

Recognising the following nine ways of approaching challenging situations when you slip into them, can help you to identify whether you are inward or outwardly focused. Or, to put it another way, whether you are connected to the truth of who you are and making decisions from that place, or are more focused on attempting to change an outcome or person and therefore disconnecting from yourself.

Chapter 7

NINE UNHELPFUL WAYS TO RECONNECT

Feel free to read the numbers that you most identify with first and then circle back to the others. There are lots of juicy thoughts here that you can drink up and digest.

1. Fixing

2. Forcing

3. Control

4. No one is coming to save you

5. Needing answers

6. Negative thinking

7. Staying stuck

8. Expectation

9. Lack of love

1. Fixing

You simply cannot fix other people, most especially when they do not want or ask for your help. Whilst being able to 'see' someone's wounds can be helpful to understand them on a deeper level, it is necessary to be cautious about turning that knowledge into only focusing on their potential. It is not your responsibility to fix them. You may find that you are starving yourself in the process.

Everyone has their own path to follow and will flow through life at their own pace. When someone appears to be suffering, it's human nature to want to help; to take the pain away. You can encourage and guide, however people must come to their own conclusions and learn their own lessons.

People are naturally encouraged to adapt or grow throughout life by different situations and experiences and it's your job to trust that process. No matter how frustrating or hard it is.

If you find yourself wanting to fix or save someone, it's a cue to acknowledge the effect the relationship is having on you. Use the pull of wanting to help as an invitation to turn inwards and consider your needs.

Allow me to illustrate this point through a story from my experience. It happened a few months after my husband had moved out, when I was still clinging to the tiniest thread of hope that we could reconnect.

After I had gone round and dropped off the food parcel, I was on alert.

My friend Emma said, "What the hell were you thinking?"

The question made me squirm in my seat as clarity rose within me.

Initially pleased with myself for my good deed, I felt light and hopeful with a spring in my step.

Then the doubt creeped in.

Every ten minutes I was checking my phone for a 'thank you.

Later, as I lay in the dark, I couldn't settle.

A whole stream of thoughts ran through my mind.

I thought I'd created an opportunity to connect and to show my affection in the hope I could begin to fix what was broken, yet I was now reeling from the self-made repercussions.

Where was the thank you? My hands, stomach and head tensed up in frustration.

Thoughts whirled.

Now came the anxious despair, washing over me like a wave - the sinking, heavy sensation filled my chest.

A quiet despondent voice spoke:

"It's not coming, is it?

"And what's worse, it won't be coming ever again."

Tears pricked my eyes, and the knots in my stomach turned to fluttering butterflies from anxiety.

Darkness wrapped around me tighter.

And then came the anger, at myself, at him, at the whole sorry situation.

How rude not to acknowledge my gesture, how heartless, how...

I vowed to myself in that moment to put myself first. To feel the pain of separation and disconnection and to prioritise healing and connecting with myself. To do something kind for me instead.

Kindness to myself now looks like checking into my inner guidance first and asking

"Who am I doing this for and what is the intention behind it?"

For example, for a few years I have been loyal to two local raw dog food suppliers. I wanted to share my custom with them so went back and forth, on alternate weeks, often going out of my way so that I would be fair about spreading out my custom. One day I caught myself fretting about running out and neither of my usual options was convenient. I realised that there must be an easier way to get what I needed without putting myself out, so I bulk ordered what I needed and got a monthly delivery. The relief and novelty when my first delivery came was wonderful.

When you feel a compulsion, a yearning to make something happen, you have been pulled off-centre. Pulled by threads of desperation, overwhelm and not knowing what to do. This can lead to rash decisions cloaked as solutions. Be sure to check in with yourself to ensure that the solutions you choose are truly in alignment with who you are and what you want. The ones that feel light and easy in your body.

TAKE FIVE PAUSE AND PRACTICE

Take a moment here to close your eyes and take some long deep breaths. Feel your body relaxing. Simply be here with your breath.

What sensations do you notice?

Do you have a sense of urgency? Breathe into it. Allow it to flow through you and take its natural course. It will subside into a sense of calm.

Keep breathing. Continue to invite calm.

Wait and breathe.

Then from this place of balance, consider your next step.

2. No forcing

When you would really like something to happen, there can be a danger of attempting to force or manipulate someone into submission. Wanting something badly can cause you to be impatient, act impulsively or disrespect boundaries.

Tension can build and may erupt in unhealthy ways like driving too fast, and behaving negatively towards innocent bystanders. The more you push, the higher the likelihood that there will be damage, breakages or pain. Attempting to force your will onto something drains your energy and can prevent you from allowing the wonderful things that are available to you to come into your life.

Forcing can lead to resentment, bitterness or martyrdom. It can be disempowering to fixate on one specific outcome and does little to serve your purpose or self-worth.

In a last-ditch attempt to spend some time with my husband and talk about his reasons for leaving, I tried to muscle in on a holiday. The holiday to Cornwall had originally been planned for all four of us plus the dogs, a family getaway to beautiful place doing activities we all enjoyed. I imagined long walks where we could chat and reconnect, time spent at the beach; surfing on a summertime sunlit glistening sea with the sparkles of light igniting the magic of love, and sitting on the sand warming our bodies and hearts.

We were in the car during one of his visits when I declared: "I'm coming with you to Cornwall. You need to give us a chance to talk and remember how nice it is to do fun things together."

I was crushed when he refused. I couldn't comprehend how he could be so unwilling.

Eventually I realised that I was disrespecting myself for begging to be loved by someone who couldn't or wouldn't love me back. Although it was horribly gut-wrenching at the time, it was a necessary wake up call. The experience showed me that I deserve better. It propelled me onto a path of healing the parts of me that attracted an unhealthy relationship and loving an emotionally unavailable man.

A mantra or saying that has really stuck with me and helped a lot throughout my healing process is:

It is what it is.

Meaning that sometimes a situation cannot be changed and so must be accepted. It is not giving in to defeat as that could be disempowering. Instead, it is loosening your grip, relaxing and allowing.

I came across the Chinese finger trap when the kids got one each in their party bags once. They are a great metaphor for a problem that can be overcome by relaxing and not trying too hard to solve it. The finger trap is a simple puzzle that traps the person's fingers, often the index fingers, in both ends of a small cylinder woven from bamboo. The typical initial reaction is to pull and try to force the fingers out, but this only tightens the trap. The way to escape the trap is to push the ends toward the middle, which enlarges the openings and frees the fingers.

When the mantra "it is what it is" popped into my mind, it was as if true love stood up and said "enough is enough, I am going to make myself known to you so you can break free from this illusion and stop trying so hard. To guide you back to your centre."

What a gift.

It took some time; it took acceptance and courage.

I realised that when it comes to true healthy love sometimes it's not clear what to look for when you haven't had the principles modelled to you. It can be quite easy to fall into accepting negative behaviours despite the niggles and red flags because you see potential. It can then be quite a feat to stop trying to hold onto and influence your version of that person. To see past the potential, no matter how well-meaning it may be.

True, wholehearted, pure love requires no force. It feels calm and grounded. It brings the best out of you and supports you to be yourself.

TAKE FIVE PAUSE AND PRACTICE

Repeat the Mantra

It is what it is,

It is what it is,

It is what it is.

Each time you say it, feel the strength that arises within you. The first time you say it, there is likely to be no sense of conviction. Once the truth of the words fully rings within you and resonates in your mind and body, the more conviction there will be behind them and the more belief you will have for them.

Notice what happens in your body.

Is there a softening? A letting go?

Notice your thoughts.

Does the tone and quality of your thoughts change?

3. No Controlling

Having self-control can be helpful when directed towards something positive you wish to achieve for yourself. Yet attempting to control others has a different quality, it erodes confidence and can make you and others feel small. Having control may seem like a tempting option to get what you want. However, adopting a domineering or aggressive stance, even attempting to control how others see you in a seemingly innocuous way, will create distance rather than connection.

Control does not feel very pleasant, and the result is likely to be an erosion of trust or rebellion from the person it is aimed at. I certainly felt that way one day when I was getting on with daily life and was suddenly faced with an unexpected correspondence.

The house was bustling with activity, the kids milling around chatting and Pepper excitedly dropping his favourite squeaky toy at my feet. He looked up at me with hopeful eyes suggesting that I would stop preparing lunch and play.

I looked down at his eager face and smiled, feeling happily content with the scene around me. A thought washed over me around how much I love family life and how blessed I am to have my children and fur babies close.

The squeaky toy hurtled down the kitchen to Pepper's delight as my attention was suddenly averted due to a familiar ping from my phone. It was a new email, so I curiously sat down at my laptop to read it and as the words came into view my heart sank, the playfulness drained away. It was like a tap turned straight onto full, the force of the water plunging downwards with vigour hard, fast and loud.

My eyes felt like they'd been stabbed with a red-hot poker at what they were being subjected to, my heart grew heavy, and my stomach knotted as my whole body sank and slumped into the chair. I sat dumbfounded with my head in my hands, gripping my hair at the content of the correspondence. Waves of fear and defiance washed over me, with a clear thought: "I will not be controlled."

I wanted to pick up the phone and let him know how unfair and downright ridiculous I thought he was being. How could he be asking for monthly reports on the kids from me because they had chosen not to speak to him - they're adults for crying out loud! Is he unaware of how the divorce process works? Thoughts screamed in my head and made me feel dizzy.

I eventually softened by reminding myself to just breathe. Bringing awareness to my breath and consciously taking some deeper inhalations and exhalations. Allowing my shoulders to gently melt down and observing the rest of my body relaxing like the domino effect.

My heart went from racing to calm and my mind from whirring to settled as I realised that I was in resistance mode and having difficulty accepting what I was faced with. I know when I am resisting something because I feel frustrated and tense. My shoulders find their way close to my ears and my jaw aches from clenching. I shook off the frustration like a dog expelling water from its coat, and understood that I was resisting viewing this from a compassionate and loving place.

I understood, painful as it was, that the behaviours and actions that I had grown accustomed to when he was in love with me, were very different now. As shocked and disappointed as I was that things had changed so radically, I knew it was still my responsibility how I responded.

One of my favourite mantras popped into my head:

I make healthy choices from a place of love.

These words are written on a card on my desk, and I see them every day. If I ever get stuck in a thought or emotion that isn't healthy for me, or I want to move forward with an action or decision and I am confused, it almost blinks at me like a neon sign. It makes me smile and reading the words instantly connects me to my heart. From the warm, loving and tender space of my heart, I am encouraged to look again at how I can choose to respond from a place of love.

I shut my laptop, took some long deep releasing breaths and made some space for the subtle loving voice of my intuition to purr away in the background until I knew what to do next.

TAKE FIVE PAUSE AND PRACTICE

Recognising resistance, preference and control

Take a few minutes and drop into the questions below. Allow any answers to arise naturally, without actively thinking or analysing the question:

What am I experiencing now?

How would I like it to be different?

Disliking what is happening and wanting what isn't here is a form of resistance, which can become a preference and then eventually control.

Honestly consider how you habitually react to this scenario and be curious about the gap between what is happening and how you would like it to be different. Can you bring some gentleness into the gap? Can you release your grip and allow for new perspectives and options to appear?

4. No one is coming to save you

As a child you rely on other people to protect you and so as an adult when your inner child is afraid, you expect and hope for an outside source to come and rescue you, take away the pain, or solve the situation. While outside sources of help such as friends and family are important additions, as an adult no one is coming to save you, except yourself.

Whilst this may feel harsh and bruising in the moment of realisation, like you have been abandoned in the cold, it truly is beautifully empowering. You can resist it, wish it was different, wallow in self-pity, and perhaps even stamp your feet. Yet when you come to understand that you are in the driving seat of your life and allow your creative mind to search for solutions, you experience the full benefits of change and can take full credit for your healing and actions moving forward.

In the early days of being separated, I fantasised about situations in which he would come and rescue me, realise what a terrible mistake he had made and resolve to make everything better. Of course, that wasn't helpful thinking, I just wanted to connect with him. It took me a while to accept that my life had changed irrevocably.   I still expected that I could somehow encourage him to reciprocate my love and kindness.

Things started to break around the house, the vacuum cleaner stopped working, the kitchen light tripped a fuse, and a tap began to drip uncontrollably. For the first time in decades, it was up to me to sort these issues out. At first, I felt quite alone, vulnerable and sorry for myself. It turned out, however, to be an opportunity for me to put my big girl pants on and reach out for help. All I needed to do was ask.

Our lovely neighbour quickly and easily resolved the vacuum issue, and my wonderful dad sorted everything else. I felt accomplished, supported and safe. I knew then that I wasn't alone; that I am never alone, and that there is always love and support around when needed or asked for. My dad and I had fun looking at kitchen taps and deciding which one would be best and then when he came to fit it, I was able to witness beautiful moments between my dad and my son Oliver.

Dad was awaiting a replacement knee operation and although fully competent to do the job, Oliver recognised that his granddad would benefit from his help. "Let me do that Granddad," Oliver said, referring to climbing under the sink, as a lovely smile grew on my dad's face. This kind of opportunity for bonding had not occurred between them before. Oliver contorted his body under the sink whilst being passed various tools, Granddad looking on guiding and explaining what he needed to do. It was such a lovely moment for me and one of the glimpses of light that kept me going in the early days of my grief.

TAKE FIVE PAUSE AND JOURNAL

Write down all the things that you need help with.

How do you feel about asking for help? What thoughts, beliefs and body sensations arise when you consider asking?

What skills do the people in your family and wider circle have?

What do you know you could do if you gave it a go?

Now look again at your list and decide what you are going to tackle yourself and who you are going to reach out to for help and support.

For example, I discovered that it was easy enough for me to mow the grass, take the rubbish to the tip and do some painting.

People love to help; let them.

5. Needing answers

All the answers you seek are within you.

Searching for answers outside of yourself rather than trusting what you think and feel gives your power away. I knew on the morning of my anniversary that something was deeply wrong. Rather than greeting me in bed with our usual morning cuppa, I found my husband downstairs fully clothed with his own cup of tea. I tried to make light of it, but I understood this act had ominous intentions and ramifications.

Sometimes you will not get the answers you seek or the sense of closure you desire, in the form of reasons from others. In those situations, you need to carry on with your life with an open heart.

In stressful situations its normal to be emotional and not to be in a neutral, logical frame of mind. Your brain will search for any answers it can find to get you back into a state of equilibrium. The answers your brain adopts or suggests may not be true or accurate. Have you ever looked at an object ahead that you can't quite make out and decided it is a particular thing, only to get closer to it and realise that you were mistaken? Like looking out to sea and mistaking buoys bobbing up and down for seals.

It's like looking at an abstract painting. You can search for hidden meanings and yet at the end of the day, it may well just be random loops of colour.

Even when you or someone else believes that there is justification for a certain behaviour, often it's a perspective in the moment that may not hold true when in a balanced state of mind. Like an impulse buy at a shop, at first you must have the thing, but then when you get home you realise that it's not needed or is unsuitable.

When something happens that pushes you to start seeing clearly, it is uncomfortable because no one likes to be disillusioned. It takes courage to determine whether you are in a fantasy and if you are not being honest. You want to believe something different; to justify it, to make it fit your model of being OK so that nothing must change. Your work is to recognise the reality. To understand what is fantasy, and where you are pretending that it's OK when it's not.

You are not responsible for anyone else's behaviour or problems; people will behave and act how they choose to. You have no control over this. It's tough yet true.

> After an awkward breakfast on my wedding anniversary, I asked my husband if he had anything planned, imagining something romantic like a woodland walk and picnic. There was nothing planned, another red flag, and so eventually he suggested we go for a drive. He took me to a rural country shopping centre where there was a café, a small woodland walk and a complimentary therapy centre that he had wanted to go into to discuss his business opportunities.

> We got out of the car and headed for the woods. I felt completely unloved and disconnected from him as he marched ahead with me trailing behind. Trudging through the mud and navigating discarded tree branches, I had the view of his back ahead of me. All the while I was hoping he would turn around, offer his hand and a warm smile. After a wander around the shops and before we had what was to be our final cuppa and cake socially as a married couple, he took me into the complimentary therapy shop and made plans to rent a room for his business.

> *"When someone shows you their true colours, don't try and paint a different picture."*
>
> - Unknown

A common thing that happens in the grief process is that you search for answers and when you cannot get the answers from the person you think holds them, you start to look to yourself instead. Unfortunately, when looking inwards in these circumstances all you will find are negative thoughts and beliefs. You may even blame yourself unnecessarily. Your inner critic comes out in full force and gnaws away at you like a dog with a bone.

For me the resounding question was: "What's so wrong with me? "A question that, after some time and self-compassionate inquiry, I could answer: nothing.

> The evening of my wedding anniversary continued to be a surreal living nightmare. Fleeing the house to find some sort of solace, I found myself alone in my car, bewildered and scared from the treacherous stormy conditions. I knew it wasn't safe to drive, even to my mum's, so I went back and resolved to talk to him, to attempt to understand where this bombshell had come from. I went upstairs and found him in bed.
>
> I stood rooted to the floor at the end of the bed and looked at him. The face looking back at me seemed almost made of stone.
>
> No smile, no warmth, just a glazed stare.
>
> I was confused, shocked, and taken aback by this sudden change in demeanour.
>
> What had happened to the soft, gentle eyes? Where had the reassuring, knowing smile gone?
>
> My mind raced, trying to make some sense of this.
>
> My stomach in knots, heat rising to my cheeks, my heart ached with sorrow and sank slowly into a deep dark hole of despair.
>
> Reaching for some sort of connection, I pleaded for some answers. I kept asking and asking, falling further into despair as silence boomed in my ears.

He rolled over, turned the light off and closed his eyes.

It was over.

He was done.

Dumbfounded, unable to move or comprehend the enormity of this gesture, I just stood, for what seemed like an eternity. I eventually walked out of the room and shut the door.

I can still see and feel the shock and disbelief of how such warmth had turned into frosty cold. I didn't recognise him anymore- it was frightening.

TAKE FIVE PAUSE AND JOURNAL

Consider the situation you would like to get some fresh insights on and write down all the facts, look at them objectively, like presenting a report.

What do you absolutely know to be true?

What is fact and what is fantasy?

What are the other person's actions telling you (not their words)?

Hold yourself with compassion if the veil of illusion comes down, it can be extremely sad to be faced with the truth. Allow yourself to grieve the version you held onto.

6. Negative thinking

Blaming, criticising and making excuses are examples of negative thinking and prevent us from taking self-responsibility. A wonderful mentor of mine and communication expert Cynthia Kane taught me that the way you talk to yourself dictates how you see the world. And that if you talk in an unkind or unhelpful way then you will view your day-to-day experiences through this same lens.

"You must take personal responsibility. You cannot change the circumstances, the seasons or the wind, but you can change yourself."

- Jim Rohn

I got a lovely job in a local leisure centre a few months after my separation. Working in a customer-facing role is a wonderful way to observe people, their attitudes and behaviours, especially during times of disappointment. There was a private party taking place in the soft play area one Friday afternoon which meant that members of the public could not gain entry for a couple of hours. One dad and his young daughter came in and asked to go into soft play and I let them know that there was a party but that they could come back later. The dad calmly acknowledged this information, looked down at his excited daughter and gently explained the situation. After a moment of disappointment, the daughter took hold of her dad's hand and quietly walked out.

Not long afterwards, a lady and her young son came in. Again, I smiled as they came up to the desk, and relayed the same information when she asked for place in soft play. However, this interaction was entirely different, the shift in energy palpable.

This lady's frustration exploded from nowhere and she angrily said that this was stupid, that other places allowed entry even when a party was going on. She spun around and with the same angry and frustrated tone, sharply told her young son that he wasn't allowed to go into soft play. When he started to cry, she yanked his arm, pulling him away saying it wasn't her fault and that he should blame us as it was our fault.

I felt quite honoured that Life had clearly demonstrated right in front of me the difference our thoughts can make in a situation. Of course, I couldn't see into the minds of these families however their outward response indicated some definite differences.

The man seemingly had a positive dialogue playing in his mind. Perhaps something like: "Oh well it would have been nice to go in, however, a child is having a lovely birthday with friends and we can come back."

On the other hand, the lady seemed to have more of a negative dialogue playing in her head. Perhaps something like: "I'm not allowed to just let my son play, why does there have to be stupid rules? I have just as much right as anyone else. It's their fault that my son is now unhappy!"

One of my all-time favourite stories to illustrate this point further is The Tale of the Two Wolves. It's said to be an old Cherokee parable.

THE TWO WOLVES

An old Cherokee Indian Chief was teaching his grandson about life.

"A fight is going on inside me," he told the young boy, *"A fight between two wolves."*

The dark one is evil — he is anger, envy, sorrow, regret, greed, arrogance, self-pity, guilt, resentment, inferiority, lies, false pride, superiority, and ego."

He continued: "The light wolf is good — he is joy, peace, love, hope, serenity, humility, kindness, benevolence, empathy, generosity, truth, compassion, and faith. The same fight is going on inside you grandson, and inside of everyone else"

The grandson pondered this for a moment and then asked: "Grandfather, which wolf will win?"

The old Cherokee smiled and simply said: "The one you feed."

Every day you make choices, and these small yet important choices define you. They are a statement of who you choose to be in this life, and what impact you will have on the world around you.

Whilst it may seem easier to feed the dark wolf; to procrastinate, complain, dismiss, ignore, and give up. There is little effort in choosing these, yes perhaps some instant gratification and yet no personal growth.

The light wolf is very different; it's harder to feed. It can be challenging, tiring and time-consuming to do things like learning, teaching, inspiring, sharing or abiding to new behaviours. These things take energy, effort, vulnerability and bravery. They take more time, and you don't usually see immediate results, they involve investment and patience.

The story continues...

The old man replied: "If you feed them right, they both win.

"You see, if I only choose to feed the light wolf, the dark wolf will be hiding around every corner waiting for me to become distracted or weak and jump to get the attention he craves. He will always be angry and will always fight the light wolf.

"But if I acknowledge him, he is happy, and the light wolf is happy, and we all win. For the dark wolf has many qualities — tenacity, courage, fearlessness, strong-willed and great strategic thinking that I have need of at times. These are the very things the light wolf lacks. But the light wolf has compassion, caring, strength and the ability to recognise what is in the best interest of all.

"You see, son, the light wolf needs the dark wolf at his side. To feed only one would starve the other and they will become uncontrollable. To feed and care for both means they will serve you well and do nothing that is not a part of something greater, something good, something of life.

"Feed them both and there will be no more internal struggle for your attention. And when there is no battle inside, you can listen to the voices of deeper knowing that will guide you in choosing what is right in every circumstance.

"Peace, my son, is the Cherokee mission in life. A man or a woman who has peace inside has everything. A man or a woman who is pulled apart by the war inside him or her has nothing.

"How you choose to interact with the opposing forces within you will determine your life. Starve one or the other or guide them both."

My separation and heartbreak enabled me to practice the lesson of the two wolves, daily. There were days, even weeks where I fluctuated between self-pity, fury, confusion and grief. I was so frustrated with myself that I still cared and yet felt so hurt. I eventually learnt that you can hold conflicting feelings within you and keep them in balance like two sides of one coin. It is possible to recognise feelings and not be pulled off-centre or weighed down by either the negative or positive. Allow them both to have space to be heard and then put them down. Ultimately, I learnt that you can love someone, care about them, or hold them in regard and not agree with their behaviours. Thus, you have the choice as to how much or little of your time or energy to give to them.

7. Staying Stuck

When you have a shock, the body knows instantly and it activates the flight, fright, freeze response, however the mind can take quite a lot longer to catch up. It takes time to assimilate what has happened and to make sense of it. This gap can be a gift to help you adjust to change. There then comes a time when you need to let go. To heal and recover.

My daughter Molly described this feeling as being "on pause", like she was going through the motions of life and yet her emotions were held in suspended animation. She asked me to take her out to dinner one night nearly a year after her dad left as she wanted to talk. She told me that the pause button had been released and realisations and questions were popping up like popping candy.

What she shared was so familiar to me and yet hearing it from her fresh insight was hard to hear. It was like all the pain and realisation I experienced quite instantly a year ago was being replayed through my beautiful, kind daughter. Her words made my heart sink like a stone as she relayed her fears and disappointments. "I'm never going to live with him or see him every day again, am I? Birthdays, Christmas and parties are going to be different."

Listening to her share was like reliving all my realisations. Like a pebble dropping into my awareness had touched my emotions and eventually rippled out to touch hers. It also filled me with such pride that she had processed her emotions and was now coming out the other side.

I described to her my way of understanding our different paces of processing by using a simile. I said: "For me, when Dad told me he was leaving it was like a big heavy bookshelf full of books containing knowledge crashing down around me, some books hitting me, the pain and understanding of the ramifications instantaneous".

I continued: "For you, I see it like the books on the bookshelf have been sliding off slowly over time. Landing on the floor open to a page for you to explore and understand. Now your insights are coming at a quicker pace with the books flying off the shelf."

I consider myself to be lucky. Lucky that I had some tools to process my emotions. At the start of my separation, my thoughts and actions were worlds apart from where I am now. Looking back, I understand that I was in a process of unravelling and transformation. A necessary part of my growth and healing. I look back with compassion and as they say hindsight is a wonderful thing.

My early strategy to hold onto my marriage was to give my husband time and space. I gave myself a deadline to give him an opportunity to reconsider. For him to discover that in fact the grass isn't greener elsewhere, it's greener where you water it which, in my mind, was at home with us. Then I extended that deadline when I reasoned to myself that he just wasn't quite ready. His actions were telling me the truth and yet when he visited, he would tell me he wasn't sure if it was all over which gave me false hope. My friends could see the truth of the situation and yet I needed to come to that conclusion on my own.

Giving people extended time, more chances, attempting to show them more love, more patience or understanding can keep you stuck. If you find yourself making excuses for them, for their actions and choices you may well be stuck. People must take responsibility for themselves; you cannot do that for them.

Getting defensive if others attempt to widen your perspective, in my experience is another indication that you are living under an illusion and avoiding moving forwards. It is a fear response when the status quo has changed and the rabbit won't go back into the hat.

Holding onto someone or the promise of something is alluring and can be admirable, however eventually sticking to your guns becomes more painful than accepting the necessity to move on. The truth is, life without flow is not life: it is stagnation, where nothing can thrive.

Attempting to control a situation is not healthy. It keeps you stuck as you are not considering the possibilities of a beautiful future and are instead fixating on something you do not have the power to change.

The only thing we have true agency over is ourselves.

People do show you their true colours, their true priorities and what they want to do through their actions. If though, you are wearing rose-tinted glasses, those colours can be distorted and confused. Taking off the glasses and looking at the actions of a person in the light of day can be illuminating.

If you have remained stuck for a while, you can choose to get unstuck. It's often just a shift in perception that will create a positive change.

HERE ARE A FEW TO CONSIDER:

You have yet to develop your Guiding Star reference point

If you are used to other people making choices and decisions for you, it's likely that you are not fully in touch with your own essence. If you try and make decisions based on what you believe is expected of you without knowing your unique desires, needs and qualities you won't be able to thrive. Going through life without a clear purpose or sense of direction is confusing and exhausting. It can make you feel apathetic, debilitated and hopeless especially when you cannot rely on certain people anymore.

Developing your Guiding Star reference point, helps you to focus on what matters to you most and make decisions that feel true and joyful to you. By developing an awareness of who you really are and what you want, you can keep on track with your new life's desires and goals. It is only possible to feel in alignment with yourself when you put your attention on what really matters to YOU, and are able to self-validate your decisions.

I did this by asking myself how I knew when I had made good decisions for myself and how they felt in my body. I also wrote down my values, skills, dreams and desires. Together the answers from this self-inquiry formed my Guiding Star reference point. Now whenever I need to make a decision and I have some doubt, I can return to these points as a personal guideline.

Your body needs to feel safe

When you are feeling stuck, adding more pleasure to your life is highly beneficial. Pleasure is what the body feels when it perceives safety, connection, nourishment and healing. It is not only an emotion or a feeling. It is a physiological process that increases your immune defences, balances your hormones, and calms your nervous system. Mentally, it increases your capacity to learn and to find solutions to your problems, your self-esteem and your capacity to bond with others.

Adding pleasure and joy to your days will help you to feel re-energised, capable and inspired. When you feel good about yourself, your creativity increases, and your passion ignites. My go-to pleasures, to name a few are; being in nature, playing with the dogs, dancing around the kitchen, a luxurious soak in the bath, a delicious meal and beautiful flowers.

You're scared of being alone or of the unknown

It could be that you have been in a relationship for such a long time that you don't know how to be comfortable being alone. The thought of the unknown — life outside of the relationship — is so daunting that you stay stuck in fantasising or wishing for a reconnection. This is a precarious mindset to have as it makes you vulnerable to going back to unhealthy patterns and missing out on beautiful future opportunities.

Being in your own space without any distractions can feel like a breath of fresh air. Treat it not as a time of loneliness, but instead an opportunity to explore your inner joy. Learn to be comfortable in your own skin and your own company before inviting others in.

At first, I was scared of the unknown, all sorts of thoughts popped into my head. Would I be truly happy again? Would I have to travel to my ideal holiday destinations alone and would I be able to achieve my dreams and goals without a partner? Then I began to notice that I enjoyed the more relaxed atmosphere around the house, the freedom of doing what I wanted, when I wanted. I could watch whatever was on TV or Netflix that interested me without checking with someone else. I could relax and read books rather than jumping up to fit into another person's schedule. A new confidence arose within me that whispered at first, then exclaimed joyfully that I can create my life and shape it into whatever I want it to be.

TAKE FIVE PAUSE AND ACT

Create a comfortable, cosy and safe space in your home and give yourself a 'Self Connection date'. You could light some candles, burn some incense, get your favourite food and drink and snuggle up to a good book. Take the opportunity to appreciate having time all to yourself. Notice that it can be very enjoyable to do whatever it is you want to do, including having full say over the TV remote!

For emotions that are stuck, watch a sad movie or play sad songs. Allow your tears to release pent up feelings. Let them flow freely to cleanse and renew, leaving you with a lovely sense of spaciousness.

8. Expectation

> *"Watering artificial flowers will never make them grow. Stop pouring your energy into one-sided relationships."*
>
> – John Mark Green

Human beings do not like the feeling of being uncertain, disillusioned or disappointed, so attempt to reduce the tension by changing beliefs or the source of information to fit the experience. This helps you to feel better and less uncomfortable with a situation that is desirable, but is out of reach or out of your hands. The psychological term for this is cognitive dissonance.

When you are married you expect the marriage to last, you expect to be loved and cherished. It is therefore natural to attempt to reduce the anxiety of potential loss by telling yourself that there is hope. You start to hope and then cling to the hope that things will improve; to expect that they will get better if you keep trying. You find ways to justify bad behaviour, give it an explanation so that you can reconcile it and therefore live with it. There may be a backstory of emotional or physical abuse and so you may justify and rationalise their behaviours because there is a reason for it and accommodate them under the circumstances.

You may tell yourself things like: "If I try harder to show them my love, then they will realise how much they are cared for and will stay/ try as well"; "Maybe I'm asking for too much"; or: "They didn't really gaslight me, they weren't thinking because they were rushing to get to an appointment."

If like me, you are empathic, you are also likely to have high expectations for yourself borne out of a need to please. Empathic people learn how to listen deeply so that they can be prepared for what other people around them may do, a type of self-preservation technique. You not only listen to words but to the use of those words, the tone of them, the body movements and the eye contact that go with them. You can interpret silence and hear everything that people don't say.

This pattern, whilst being very beautiful in other circumstances, entrenches you in perpetuating state of 'trying' and 'fixing', and can plague you with confusion. Once you have earned more money, lost weight or kept the house spotless, you find that the goalposts have been moved further away. Calling this out is OK and yet may be scary.

Along with the expectation and hope is an underlying fear. Fear that there will never be someone better or that you will be alone forever without a partner. This fear is an old pattern, stemming from previous conditioning such as having authoritarian parents, experiencing abuse or lack of emotional support when you were young. Somewhere along the line you got the message that you had to be 'good' or 'pleasing' to receive love. This belief then drives you to work harder, justify and explain away, sadly against your otherwise better judgement and intuition.

Managing expectations can protect you.

People do not tend to change. Once you are aware that the person you hoped they were is an illusion and that they are not amenable to change, managing your expectations is a healthy way to move on. Remembering that in a one-sided or unhealthy relationship they are unlikely to take self-responsibility, recognise that they are hurting you, or want to learn how to emotionally connect is knowledge that can you free. The truth will always set you free, even if it is uncomfortable or bitterly disappointing.

Check-in with yourself and ask:

Is your kindness a choice or is it a trauma response?

Are your people-pleasing tendencies leaving you tending to people who give you the bare minimum? Are you giving them your fullest attention with the hopeful expectation that it will be reciprocated?

Is your wish to believe you are a 'happy family' blinding you from the truth?

9. Lost love

Love is a beautiful energy that flows like water. If allowed to flow unimpeded it can be life-giving, refreshing and quenching. When faced with obstacles it can navigate them with relative ease, finding the smallest of cracks to flow through. However, when love is blocked it can damn up inside you causing pain and suffering.

Love is always a part of you. It is not something you lose. When a relationship ends or a loved one dies, the love you feel does not automatically stop — you can't turn the flow off like a water tap. Grief is love that has nowhere to go. Without an outlet love, like water, can stagnate, turning it from fresh to pungent. It becomes the pain, self-doubt and apathy you carry around with you. A way to resolve this uncomfortable feeling is to direct the flow of love inwards by practicing open-heartedness; self-love and self-compassion.

Self-worth is a large part of love. Self-worth is the inner sense of being good enough, worthy of love and belonging. It's about truly valuing yourself.

"*I don't love you anymore*", are hard words to hear, probably the most heart-wrenching words that anyone can say to another person. When these words were uttered to me, it knocked the stuffing out of me and, because I'm human, I took them to heart. I believed they meant I was unlovable. Not only that, I took those words and made a meal out of them; I took them out for dinner and entertained them. "I don't love you anymore", was plated up and tasted like "I'm flawed, I've done something wrong and I don't deserve to be loved for who I am".

I went to town to figure out what had caused this dramatic shift, with the spotlight resolutely focused on me. At first my approach was self-deprecating, judgemental and blaming. I searched for all the ways I was at fault. I even spent some painful weeks questioning reality. Thoughts spiralling around my mind acted like a borer, deepening my black hole of despair; "Was it real?" "Did he ever love me?" "Was it all a lie?"

Viewing myself as a tender and loving person, I chose to show love despite it not being reciprocated. I hoped that I could show that love can conquer all. What I didn't realise then was that it does; the difference is where you choose to focus that love. I was focusing love outwards to someone who no longer wanted to receive it whilst neglecting the most important person — me.

Acceptance led me to understand what I would like your beautiful heart to hear: When they loved you, they really loved you — it was real. When they ended the relationship and they left you that was also real. Both are true, both are valid.

Love is an energy and energy cannot be destroyed, it simply changes form.

My invitation is for you to take this as your opportunity to value yourself way more than you already do. To cultivate a practice of self-love. As you improve your self-worth you can have what's possible: a great relationship with yourself — and with another. To love and to be loved.

Over time, I gained a more balanced perspective. I realised that relationships are two-way streets. I had found myself in a cul-de-sac which seemed cosy for a while until it became clear that I had blocked off the full flow of love that was available to me.

Ask yourself: *If I treated myself like someone I truly loved, what would I do?*

Chapter 8

PRESS THE PAUSE BUTTON

Activating calm with breathing and meditation

Breathing plays an important role when it comes to your physical and emotional state. When you are in a state of stress your breathing tends to be faster which, in turn, stimulates anxious thoughts. It's like listening to fast music, which is great for getting pumped up for exercise, but not so great if you are already feeling overwhelmed and your body and mind are crying out for some peace.

I have found remembering to use my breath as a way of self-soothing incredibly useful. Your breath is always available day or night, and practicing slowing down the breath offers relief quickly. Introducing a sense of calm and slowing everything right down when you are feeling overwhelmed, shocked or anxious gives a wonderful sense of reassurance and release from anxiety and stress. Giving yourself this opportunity to pause is a beautiful gift to yourself. Once you learn to self-regulate, it means that you take your power back, enabling you to feel better without relying on others which is a form of co-dependency.

By intentionally slowing down your breathing, your body and mind have the chance to reclaim some calm, to soothe you.

TAKE FIVE PAUSE AND PRACTICE

Breathing Practice

Use the following steps to slow down your breathing and notice how your mind and body can relax.

Step 1. Sit comfortably or lie down

Step 2. Take a breath in for four seconds

Step 3. Hold the breath for two seconds

Step 4. Release the breath for six seconds

Step 5. Pause briefly before breathing again

Step 6. Practice, practice, practice.

Tips

When you first have a go at slowing down your breathing, it may be challenging. Play around with it and see what works for you. You may find using a three in, one hold and four out breathing cycle easier to begin with. See what works for you, as long as you are slowing down your breathing as much as you can comfortably, and the out-breath is longer than the breath in.

When doing this breathing practice, make sure that you are breathing into your belly rather than your chest. You can check this by placing one hand on your belly and one hand on your chest. The hand on your stomach should rise when you breathe in and fall when you breathe out. Be patient with yourself as you practice, you will improve over time.

Practice slow breathing once or twice a day, initially at a time when you can relax and are free from distraction. The aim is then to use this skill when you notice you are having a hard time emotionally to activate a calm state, wherever you are and whatever you are doing.

Meditation

I have practiced meditation for 25 years and it is the foundational practice for all the other modalities I have learnt to grow and develop as a person. Whilst I am by no means an expert meditator who sits in the lotus position for hours, I do reap the benefits of the practice. Meditation has given me access to insights and self-awareness, catching negative and positive thought patterns and beliefs. Meditation often gives me respite from whirling thoughts and leaves me feeling calmer and self-assured.

What your mind pays attention to and how it does that contribute to your emotional and physical state. Much of the time the thoughts playing in your mind and what you are experiencing just happen. This is often referred to as being on autopilot or being mindless. Mindfulness encourages you to notice that mind full of thoughts and their quality — are they positive, negative or neutral? Meditation, the formal practice of mindfulness, helps you to recognise that thoughts are not reality. You discover that it's more useful to avoid fighting against them and instead allow them to flow.

Catching your thoughts and feelings and being able to take a step back from what you are experiencing without getting too caught up in them involves being mindful. Mindfulness means paying attention to the present moment and not judging whatever you notice is happening. Not trying to stop and change whatever you are experiencing. Simply watching.

Mindfulness requires you to be aware of what's around you and how your body feels. Meditation is a practice that reels in your thoughts to calm the mind. Meditation is a wonderful way of echoing the truth that you are enough. It is a practice that relies on what is already inside you.

You are not your thoughts.

Your thoughts, the voice in your head is not who you really are. Thoughts come and go, arise and fall away. There's an awareness behind the thoughts that watches them come and go — this is you.

Knowing this can be such a relief because it shows you that you don't have to take your thoughts so seriously. Meditation is a place where you can experience yourself differently. An opportunity to create some distance between yourself and the thought patterns, beliefs and stories that contribute to your suffering.

Meditation involves noticing when your attention has wandered away from the present moment and gently redirecting your attention back to the here and now. It is not a way of attempting to control your thoughts and feelings or to make them go away. Instead, it is allowing them to be present within you and at the same time choosing to shift your attention back to the present moment.

There's a Zen saying that goes:

"You should sit in meditation for twenty minutes a day. Unless you're too busy, then you should sit for an hour."

Taking time out and pressing the pause button helps you to reset, especially on the most chaotic or stress-filled days. The best way to take care of the future is to be in the present moment, now. Sometimes you just need to BE for a while, not fixing, not trying to make anything happen. It's a moment-by-moment choice that becomes a way of being. And over time things change.

When you are distracted, you can easily get caught up in thinking and get lost in streams of thought, even falling into the stream The good news is that your mind will settle if you allow it, just like water will settle if left undisturbed. The constant involvement with thinking is what keeps it unsettled. The more you practice meditation, you are likely to find that it's more often the mind that is causing you to suffer and not reality.

According to Kundalini Yoga there are three aspects of mind: positive, negative and neutral.

The positive mind thinks about positive outcomes, where you expect the best. It is your inner eternal optimist.

The negative mind thinks about the worst-case scenario, the just-in-case. It does this to protect you and is an extension of vulnerability.

The neutral mind thinks of the bigger picture. It's calm and open, it allows life and the source of love to speak to you.

It is the neutral mind that is cultivated when you practice mindfulness and meditation regularly.

There are many different meditations you can practice and many resources that go deeply into the benefits of meditation which are beyond the scope of this book. To get you started I will share a common meditation practice.

Your breath is something that is always with you and typically you are not aware of so it until you focus on it and so is a useful point of focus to begin with.

To recap, the formal practice of mindfulness is meditation, and it is a way you can train yourself to be more aware of where your attention goes and gets caught and to redirect your attention to the present moment using a focus of your choice.

Meditation steps

1. Start by finding a comfortable position. You can either:

   Sit cross-legged on a cushion, allow your back to be straight, keep your eyes closed or half closed and fold your hands comfortably on your lap.

   If you prefer you can sit in a chair with your feet flat on the floor and your hands resting on your lap.

   Or you can lie on the floor, on your back with your legs straight out, a few inches apart and your arms at your sides, preferably with palms facing up.

2. Check in with how you are now; your thoughts, emotions, and sensations.

   Ask yourself, what am I experiencing right now? What's my internal weather? What thoughts are around, what feelings and body sensations do you notice? Allow yourself to acknowledge and observe these experiences without judgement and without attempting to change them or make them go away. Practice this for 30 seconds to one minute

3. Now spread out your focus to become aware of your breathing.

Focus on the sensations of your breath as you inhale and exhale. Notice the cool air entering your nostrils as you breathe in, and the warm air being released as you exhale. Notice your belly or ribcage rising and falling. If your mind wanders, notice what thoughts, feelings or sensations it has focused on without trying to change them or making them go away. Acknowledge their presence by saying: "I see you/ I feel you, and now I am going to refocus on my breath." Then let go of your attention and focus back on your breath. Do this for one to two minutes.

4. Now spread out your focus from the breath to become aware of the whole body.

Allowing the body to be just as it is. Spread out your focus to any activity within the mind and allowing it to be just as it is. Becoming aware now of the space surrounding the body, any sense of warmth or coolness, the sounds around you and the ground beneath you. Open your eyes gently and noticing the shapes and colours around you. Gradually opening up to your whole experience in this moment.

5. Take a moment to reorient yourself and continue with the activities of your day.

Remember that it is not possible to have a blank mind. Your mind will wander, that's what minds do. The practice of meditation is to gently escort the mind back to the present and the task at hand, for example to focus on the breath or a mantra. To cultivate awareness of where your mind has wandered to and bring it back.

THE ART OF RECEIVING

You can't breathe out and not in again.

Take a moment to consider this.

There is a balance to everything upheld by the universal law of equilibrium. In modern-day society however, this law is not widely acknowledged or taught. You are taught about the virtues of giving but not the receiving so it's hard to take things in. Giving more than receiving has become normalised and therefore the damage this does is not easily recognised. It is perpetuated down family lines and then into your relationships.

If you have been in a relationship or situation that was not reciprocal, that was unhealthy and causing it to be out of balance, then you are likely to have given much more than you received. You may be used to pouring yourself out and not being filled up. I want you to know that you deserve more, and that it is safe to ask for more. And more than just enough.

Practising the art of receiving gently builds up your receiving muscles. You are on this Earth to thrive; to enjoy life, and you cannot do that if you are constantly in deficit. Receiving by noticing how delicious it feels to take a breath in is one way, another is connecting to yourself through meditation.

Here are a few more:

- Saying thank you when someone compliments you and fully taking it in.
- Allowing people to help you, even if you can do it yourself you don't have to!
- Choosing to believe that you deserve all good things.

When I eventually told my good friend Samantha, who had been friends with us both for several years, that my husband had left and the way he did, she was sad. She wasn't just sad about the situation, she was sad that I hadn't confided in her sooner. She felt she had missed an opportunity to support me when I was in turmoil and pain, and didn't like the thought that she could have been there for me if I had let her know.

Even though I knew how much of a good friend she was and how much love she brought to all of us (dogs included), I couldn't face telling her because I felt ashamed. Looking back, I was also in shock and living in a kind of trauma bubble that took me some time to emerge from, even so it was the thoughts around not being good enough that made me resist receiving her kindness.

The wonderful visceral sense of being loved and cared for that I felt as soon as I reached out and received support was deeply nourishing. Through my amazing friends and family, I was able to see that there was no need to be ashamed and that they wanted to help me because of who I am. I was not defective, I was not unworthy, in fact the complete opposite.

PART 3

Expand and connect

Chapter 9

EXPANSION — RECONNECTION TO YOURSELF

"How did you do it?"

"How did you take your power back?" was the very thoughtful question my friend Lesley posed.

The answer gathered in my head like pieces of a jigsaw puzzle coming into view. I knew I had all the pieces and had not yet put them together until that moment of inspired clarity. They shuffled in my mind, found their right places, and suddenly the full picture was formed. It was like completing a game of solitaire on a computer when you realise you've won. You can choose to allow the computer to finish the game. It then feverishly sorts all the remaining cards and puts them on the correct piles and finishes enthusiastically by offering you congratulations with a triumphant "dadaah!"

I realised that if I had a map of how I did it; how I went from shock, disbelief and despair to understanding, acceptance and peace, that meant I could find the pattern and the connecting pieces for you as well. This realisation filled me with excitement and contentment — the same feeling I get when I see the snowdrops peeking through the ground in my garden in late January, early February. Seeing these little shoots heralds the coming of the spring, lighter days, optimism and opportunities for more play after the darkness of winter.

How did I do it — my map

After the initial shock of separation, I gathered as much information as I could, feeling into what was nurturing for me to listen to and keep and what was unhelpful, in an attempt to understand what was going on and why.

As my husband said that he *"did not have to answer"* any of my questions, I didn't have much to go on to accept and make peace with this sudden, unexplained devastation that had ripped through my life like a tornado without warning. I knew I needed to process it and yet didn't know where to start.

At first, I was outwardly focused on what I could do or be differently to repair our relationship. The frustration and hope of making everything OK again consumed me. All I could think about was how to save my marriage and the life I knew. I clung onto it tight, like a baby gripping onto your finger with all its might. I realised later that it was a blessing that he refused to give me any answers because the answers I needed were never going to come from him. It was me that had them all along.

I read book after book; trawling the pages for clues on how to repair our relationship; "How To Save Your Marriage", "Seven Keys to a Happy Marriage" and "Atlas of the Heart" to name just a few. Yet as I read them, a theme emerged that I was not expecting.

At the same time, my daughter came across a catchy mantra that she shared with me, and it stuck. Whenever I fell into doom and gloom, the words were repeated back to me like an enthusiastic cheerleader; in a playful, repetitive, inspiring ditty kind of tone that lifted me out of my funk.

"Rejection is protection."

"Rejection is protection, rejection is protection, rejection is protection."

Those words comforted me and created curiosity within me as I questioned: "What am I being protected from?" And as time went on and my attempts to heal the rift in my marriage failed, I knew that I was being protected from going backwards. I understood that not all storms come to disrupt your life, some come to clear your path.

I wasn't expecting to discover that there are ingredients to a happy marriage that I hadn't been experiencing and that you can indeed have your cake and eat it too. When I felt full and satiated from my profound inquiry, I had a good sense as to what hadn't been working in my marriage. I also realised what I need to feel connected, nurtured and loved, and that it was OK to want those things.

I went on to listening to my feelings and then deeply exploring my emotions; skills that I have honed over recent years. Like many people, perhaps including yourself, I had always shied away from truly expressing my feelings and therefore my needs for fear of some kind of negative response or consequence.

For example, in 2014 I was so worried about telling my parents that I was quitting my job and going self-employed that I wrote an email outlining my reasons! Even though I was following my joy, it was a daunting prospect to share and carry out.

The difference between feelings and emotions however is that feelings are mental reactions and can be hidden, whereas emotions are physical states that can pop up at any moment as well as being so deep that it can take a lifetime to connect with and understand them.

Emotions can seem overwhelming and scary, like a black hole that you could get sucked into whilst kicking and screaming and never remerge. I have discovered that the best way to work with emotions is to allow them the space they need to fully flow. When you have experienced and felt the emotion, sat with it without running away, it then has a chance to dissipate. Emotions or e-motions are energy in motion and need to flow. If they stagnate and get stuck, they can become unknown entities that are scary until they are exposed to the clarifying light of day.

To start expressing my emotions, I had to identify what they were and label them. Then feeling those emotions without judgement and accepting that they were there as messengers sent to help me not hinder me.

I discovered exploring my feelings and writing them down layer after layer was very cathartic and healing. Each time I explored my emotions and feelings, the thoughts and beliefs I had attached to them, and what stories I was telling myself, I had greater understanding and compassion for myself.

I decided to write in a journal every day so that I could feel the relief of releasing my thoughts. To begin with all writing happened sat tucked up in bed, my safe cosy space. I got a cup of tea and a glass of water just in case I was there for quite a while, ensured tissues were handy, and got out my journal and pen.

I dated the page at the top and poured out my thoughts. Angry thoughts, despairing thoughts, hopeful thoughts. Dating the page helped me to go back and evaluate and assess my progress. To help me recognise changes in my perception towards myself and my experiences.

I gained so many insights by making space to write. For example, it amazed me how you can get so used to and accepting of the behaviours of others, especially when they are not healthy or kind. Often in the midst of life, words and deeds go under the radar only to be flagged when either you decide, or life nudges you, to be open to truly listening.

For a long time, I was in denial. I sugar-coated the unpleasant things and often blamed myself instead of facing the truth of the situation. I tried to prove myself worthy in the hope of being recognised. Only when looking back with fresh eyes and a self-loving heart did I distinguish the reality. I appreciate that hindsight is a wonderful thing and so having a record of your thoughts and feelings to look back on from a place of self-compassion can be very healing and liberating.

I wrote in my journal every day, mainly in the morning, as well as when thoughts popped randomly into my head. Some days I was pensive and calm, I took time to consider what I truly thought. I would tap my pen end to end on the journal from which clarity arose, just like the sound and rhythm of a shamanic drum creates the space for new inquiry and insight.

Other days I wrote through gritted teeth frantically and angrily as smoke almost rose from the page. If I knew that I had a lot to release, I would then take a separate piece of paper and write a letter, pouring out my thoughts and then burning it. Watching the paper set alight and the fire curling the words on the page with a red glow, reducing it to ash helped me to release them and the pain they described to the Universe. I knew that holding that anguish inside my body was toxic to me and this ritual made space for new, healthier thoughts to arise.

Days where I was a puddle of tears, gulping big breaths and sobbing my heart out were particularly tough and yet were very cleansing. Big realisations and the particularly thoughtless actions of others brought up a sense of being unsafe that turned on the tap. In those moments I would use my tools for self-soothing, to let myself know that I was fundamentally safe and OK. For example, I would put one hand on my heart and one hand on my stomach and repeat this mantra:

I am safe,

I am loved,

All is well.

As I repeated those words over and over and felt the warmth of my hands soothing me, the big gulping gasps for air turned to slow deep breaths and my heart went from galloping to a gentle rhythmic beat. My body unfurled from a tense bent-inward position to a straighter, softer and more confident posture.

From that space, I wrote about what I needed and wanted. I was renewed in my resolve to learn and grow from this experience and not to be bitter or broken by it. My writing had a pattern to it and when I look at my journals now, I can see the trajectory my healing journey took.

It started with themes around questioning what am I going to do? Concerns about everything I had lost or was going to lose: security, love, money, our home.

Then thoughts shifted to how unfair it seemed that my world had been turned upside down and it was not my choice, not my decision.

There was confusion, despair and grief, missing connection, fear of the future, disappointment, hope and then acceptance.

Writing was a huge comfort to me, and I was able to express a lot. Eventually my writing practice moved from my bed to the dining room table where it has remained. The change from being cocooned in my bedroom to a more communal space in the house signalled a positive shift in healing for me.

One of my biggest challenges in the early months was talking about what had happened, even to those who were closest to me. I was utterly mortified. I was extremely sheepish about reaching out to talk or let people know about the dramatic change in my life. I imagined that people would wonder what was wrong with me. I truly thought that I would be judged as being defective in some way.

Luckily the road rose up to meet me and my amazing mum, family and wonderful friends rallied around and bolstered me. They acted like scaffolding around a sacred monument, holding me up, protecting me, bringing food, and chocolate, and soothing me with their words of kindness and wisdom.

How does that make you feel?

It was during a weekend retreat to Scotland to visit my business mentor Mandy that another guest and business colleague Rachael asked me a profound question. The answer to which was like a key unlocking the door to my future happiness.

I wasn't sure if I could face going to the retreat at first — I was still in shock. The trip had been planned for quite a while and Mandy reassured me. She suggested to treat the time away as a nurturing retreat. I could relax, be creative and be in the company of some great women. No expectations. No cooking. Being taken care of in a beautiful space, in a gorgeous part of the country.

I went along and I am so glad that I did. True to her word Mandy made my whole stay comfortable and easy-going. She listened to my woes, offered words of wisdom, fed me gorgeous food and gently started my healing process through helping me create a series of empowering multimedia art pieces. Being in her presence and watching her work was inspiring.

One morning after a walk, I was in the dining room with Rachael waiting for everyone else to come in for an activity. We were talking about my situation at home and how for several months leading up to my husband's departure I had felt unsupported and put down by some of his comments about my business plans.

Rachael reflected back to me that I seemed disheartened by this and that I had been putting up with negative energy that was making me feel small and contracted. She then invited me to feel how it would be different to do what I wanted to do, with encouragement and support.

"How does that make you feel?" she said. *"To allow yourself to be fully you?"*

Suddenly, seemingly out of nowhere I felt my whole being lift and rise, upwards and outwards. A lightness, an expansion, like I grew ten feet taller with a great big Cheshire cat grin on my face. This visceral sensation of body and mind surprised me, it was a wonderful feeling of hope and joy. Yet it scared me. I knew in that moment a choice was on the horizon. A choice I would need to make peace with, so that I could hold that feeling of expansiveness and freedom. I would need to let my husband go.

The promise of that profound, uplifting sensation stayed with me. It was like I had walked through the wardrobe into Narnia, a whole new magical world. I knew that I could return there and eventually I did.

After three months, once the shock had settled and I could eat properly again, I found the courage to feel the fear of the unknown and allowed myself to dream about what my new life would look like. I resolved to use this experience as an opportunity to follow what makes my heart sing, to flow through life using my skills and tune into guidance if I got stuck.

I also knew in my bones, at the very core of me, that I had an abundance of love to give and share. I knew that I couldn't and didn't want to keep all that love to myself. I decided to employ love and use it in every decision and action I took. To be guided by love.

Once my emotions were more balanced and I had a clearer idea of who I am and what I want, my creativity really began to rise, and I knew that writing a book would be a great way for me to express myself and everything I have learnt. I was back in the driving seat of my life; the ruler of my world again, autonomous and in contented alignment. And with the added attraction of helping others with my humble offering, a book felt like a good way to spread my love into the world.

I also challenged myself to do new things and activities that I would have previously relied on other people to do. Small things built my confidence like collecting parcels from depots that meant I had to navigate my least favourite roundabouts. Picking up my son in the middle of the night from a party when he called for assistance, and a different kind of challenge: hotpod yoga.

I tested myself. Felt the fear and acted.

At times I was surprised at the ways my heartbreak and separation had affected me, how much it had knocked my confidence and caused me to feel vulnerable and uncertain in surprising situations. When my emotions popped up unexpectedly although they initially phased me, I used the tools I have learnt to support me. Over time I was able to cultivate deeper levels of inner strength to ride the waves of fear. One wave at a time.

Imagine a friendly, open-minded and welcoming group of people inviting you into a warm and cosy space to relax. No problem you would think. My system thought otherwise!

> Inside the pod was lovely, it was dark except for some pretty string lights and set up with everything I needed. Mats, blocks, blankets. Gentle music was playing, and a lovely aroma wafted from a diffuser. I had my water and fluffy socks and my lovely friend Samantha beside me. The dome shape of the dark purple pod was cocooning and high enough not to be claustrophobic.

> Then the facilitator zipped us in, snug as a bug. The sound of the zip closing the pod and shutting off my exit caused a ripple effect in my mind and body. Suddenly the darkness felt scary, the uncertainty of what was going to unfold started my mind racing, the sound of the fans loud in my ears, the heat seemed to rise as high as the Sahara Desert. I felt trapped inside with a large group of strangers with the expectation to release and relax.

> I wanted to run away, yet the wiser part of me started to whisper reassurances. "Take a sip of water. Close your eyes and breathe. Press your thumb and forefingers together to move the energy. Lay down, feel the support of the Earth holding you."

> As I did so, I felt more in control and calmer.

> When I sat up and opened my eyes, I leant over to the kind-eyed facilitator and said: "What if I freak out?"

> With a knowing smile, he gently said" "It's just a zip, if you need to leave you can. For now, how about you have a go at riding the waves of discomfort and using your breath."

That extra pep talk soothed my worried inner child and I was then able to watch my thoughts and body have moments of fear and met them with breathing slowly and deeply.

I settled into the class after a while, my shoulders gently melted down from my ears inviting my whole body to follow suit and soften. I noticed the areas where I was holding tension like my jaw and face and let go. My mind stopped racing and became quiet. The sounds in the pod went from a cacophony to focused as I tuned into the instructions being given.

In the end I felt restored; warm, loose in my body, and my mind free from chatter. I really enjoyed the experience and had a big sense of achievement for having stayed and worked through my initial discomfort.

LOOKING THROUGH THE NINE STAR KI LENS

Everyone journeys through life's challenges according to their unique blend of circumstances, skills and tools, attachment styles, past experiences and archetypal patterns. Your Nine Star Ki archetypes can go a long way to helping you discover and recognise how you are likely to think, feel and respond to stressful situations. If you are out of balance, they show you how to come back into equilibrium so that you can handle these situations with grace.

Reconnecting with my truth, the essence of who I am and how I show up in the world was made easier when I used the Nine Star Ki Guiding Stars or energetic archetypes as a guide. Knowing who I am through this lens helps me to be kinder and less judgemental towards myself.

The archetypes are on a continuum or scale, full of different variations of personalities. Each archetype can be described in its main form and then further defined by its characteristics.

Let's take water as an example.

Water can take many forms, but its essential purpose is to support life — without it you would not survive. On one side of the scale, water can be large swelling waves that crash down and batter the sand; powerful and ferocious. On the other end of the scale, majestic icebergs; cold, hard and travelling down deep into the sea. In between you can find bubbling brooks, snowflakes, waterfalls, calm deep lakes, and trickling streams.

Water is most useful to us though when it is in a still and calm state so that it can be utilised for drinking and bathing in.

Whilst all varieties are welcome, residing in the middle of the continuum offers the best opportunity for feeling balanced and centred; that you have autonomy in your life and are not being held to ransom by your fears or carried away by your ego. If you spend too long at the extremes it can be detrimental and like most things in life, its preferable to aim for the middle ground. Like Goldilocks and the porridge: not too sweet not to sour, just right!

You will travel along the continuum at different points in your life, even fleeting moments in your day. Being aware of what state you are in and how to get back into equilibrium is a skill and requires practice. Once you are aware of what to look for you are halfway there — awareness is key.

Once I understood the full scope of who I am at my core, in my natural, healthy and balanced state, I recognised what was guiding me. It is me. It is you. It has been this way the whole time. It's the version of you that is connected to the Universal life-giving, life-affirming force of Love. The version that is open to being authentic and whole.

RECONNECTING TO YOUR WHOLENESS

When you experience a significant change in your life, like a breakup or ending of a friendship it comes with a sense of loss. That there is a piece that is missing. This can arise from a tendency to put people on pedestals in your mind. Because you perceive them to have more of a particular quality than you have, when they are no longer a big part of your life you feel the absence of it.

I always perceived my ex-husband as adventurous; he would go surfing, climbing, and drive to far-flung places just to explore. When we were no longer going on these adventures with him, I worried that life would become boring.

What I did not give myself credit for was that I am adventurous in different ways. I showed my adventurous side when I took a risk and became self-employed. I am adventurous with my ideas, new ways of thinking and bucking the trend like organising a baby naming ceremony instead of a traditional christening for our daughter long before they were popular.

When someone or something is not connected to you anymore, it does not mean that you personally have broken apart or are no longer whole. You were and are always whole. It is your self-awareness and self-worth that may need to be repaired so that you can reconnect with all the forgotten or disowned parts of you.

RECOGNISING WHOLENESS EXERCISE

Write down a trait that you admire in someone.

It could be having a sense of humour, being kind, playful, assertive, or a great communicator.

Underneath this trait, write down all the ways that you display this quality, recognising that there are many variations to each one.

Where can you take full ownership of the quality?

Notice now how differently you feel about yourself.

Write down what you now recognise about yourself that's different to before.

Chapter 10

EMOTIONS

Feelings matter, you matter

How you feel is important. Allowing your feelings to be a guide enables you to align with the truth of who you are. The 'You-ness' of You, your inner being. Your feelings show you who you are allowing yourself to be right now and are highlighted by your thoughts. Your feelings guide you towards discerning whether your thoughts match up with your intentional way of being.

My intentional way of being is to be guided by love and so whenever I have thoughts that are less than loving I reach for kinder, more compassionate or loving perspectives. This is a process and involves practice.

When I notice an uncomfortable sensation, I pause to listen to its message. Emotions — especially triggering ones, signal to your body and soul that there is room for a lesson, healing, growth or observation is needed. It's not always immediately obvious what the message is, in fact it often takes some excavation, patience and self-compassion to unveil the treasure. All emotions are absolutely valid and are there to be felt, heard and understood.

Emotions are energy in motion or e-motion and must be able to flow freely and be expressed for you to stay in a healthy balance. Being in balance and grounded means that you are not so easily swayed or knocked by uncomfortable or triggering events, and you can bounce back or come back to your centre — the core of you — more quickly and easily should you lose your way.

In nature, willow trees are a good example of this. On windy days they can be bashed by the wind and rain causing them to bend and sway and yet if their roots are strong, they come back to standing again.

Emotions are reactions linked to your fight, flight and freeze response and are largely unconscious until something happens to trigger them. All emotions tell you something about yourself and your situation. They are often accompanied by negative thoughts, which may fly under the radar until you consciously choose to notice and catch them. Triggering events can be small or more significant. The term 'triggered' refers to having an emotional reaction to an event that reminds you of something that previously made you feel unsafe.

Your emotions start as sensations in the body whereas your feelings are generated from your thoughts about those emotions. Being aware of your emotions, feelings and core needs help you to feel calm, peaceful and happy. Emotions act as a guide for you. They alert you to your inner landscape. They invite you to explore what is going on deep inside you. To connect inwards and observe the state of your inner weather as well as your physical landscape.

Being aware and mindful, for example, when stress is creeping up on you, that you are holding onto an irritation or that you are all well with the world is important information. Checking in on your feelings is not widely taught, yet it is so beneficial to maintaining your vitality. Knowledge is power. Awareness is key.

Once you are aware of and understand what is going on within you and what steps you can take to improve it, you have sovereignty over yourself. You have taken back the wheel and are in the driving seat of your life. Being aware of your underlying emotions enables you to make the next link between what you truly need and want. To understand what your non-negotiables are in life so that you can conquer and then maintain what is important to you.

TAKE FIVE PAUSE AND PRACTICE

Inner landscape check-In

I invite you to take an inner landscape inventory, to survey the land of your body and mind.

Stop any activity that you are doing. Put down your pen, phone or laptop. Sit or stand comfortably and close your eyes.

What do you immediately notice?

How does your body feel? Are there any obvious tensions?

What thoughts can you catch yourself thinking? Are they positive, worried, self-deprecating?

Does pausing give you relief?

Take a few deep breaths now.

How does that alter your inner landscape?

Breathing or breath is the bridge between body and mind. It helps you to connect the two. It assists you in regulating your nervous system from parasympathetic to sympathetic. From stressed and on high alert for threats to calm, peaceful and safe.

When your nerves feel jangled, your stomach is in knots and your mind is like spaghetti the easiest and most effective way to bring some comfort and soothing is to simply be and breathe.

Checking in regularly throughout the day is a wonderful way of tracking your progress from catastrophic to calm, from tense to tender and panic to peace.

THE THREE EMOTIONAL SYSTEMS

Understanding how you can manage and balance your emotions helps to turn your focus towards cultivating self-compassion and self-love. This is because when you know which emotional system you are currently using, you can choose to step out of it or stay with it. Being aware of your emotional state enables you to consider whether what you are thinking or doing serves you or how it is not serving you.

How do you know if your emotions are out of balance and need regulating? Professor Paul Gilbert answered this question by developing the Three Emotional Systems model, using neuroscience research and receiving a Knighthood for this valuable and insightful work.

The model describes how your evolved brain has three emotional systems that you switch between and that each one is associated with different regions of the brain and different chemistry.

The Three Emotional Systems are:

- A threat and self-protection system
- A drive and resource-seeking system
- A soothing and contentment system

The threat system is always on the lookout for threats to your safety and that of your loved ones. It aims to protect you by preparing you to run away from physical danger. It is also activated by non-physical threats such as worrying or not being able to do things. It is connected to feelings of anger, fear, anxiety and disgust. Your body produces adrenaline when you are in this system.

If your threat system dominates the others, you can often feel under threat, on guard or constantly anxious. When you are in threat mode, your thinking becomes very narrow and negative, and your mind becomes unable to move out of its negative narrow focus. It is difficult to think rationally in threat mode because this type of thinking involves sophisticated processing and time. In threat mode your thinking is quick and reactive. That's why it's important to be gentle with yourself when you are experiencing distressing emotions; your mind was not designed to think rationally when under stress or in danger.

The drive system is focused on getting the resources needed for you to survive and thrive. It aims to motivate you and spur you on to try new things, to achieve goals and is reward-based: you feel good afterwards, like experiencing those joyful 'high five' moments. It is connected to feelings of excitement, focus and wanting.

Your body produces dopamine when you are in this system, the effect of which can be mimicked by stimulants such as caffeine.

If you spend most of your time in drive, it can send you into overdrive, the compulsion to do more and do better and you can get trapped in "I must achieve, I must do better, I must do, do, do." Then when something stops you from achieving, you can become distressed and self-critical — this can then push you into threat mode.

The soothe system helps you to manage stress and bond with others. It has a calming influence on both the threat and the drive systems, helping to quieten them down when they are overactive. It relates to feelings of contentment, safety and connection to others. You can tell when you are in the soothe system when you are chilled out, feeling safe, calm and content.

Your body produces opiates and oxytocin — the feel-good chemical — in this state. The soothe system can only operate when there are no threats to your safety and when you have sufficient resources for the time being. When this system is activated, you can soothe yourself in times of difficulty and suffering. To feel safe includes feeling able to reach out for support from friends, family and sources of help.

Experiences of kindness, care and compassion stimulate this system. Investing in yourself by spending time on activities that make you feel content, safe and cared for brings your soothe system online balancing your emotions and improving your well-being.

TAKE FIVE PAUSE AND JOURNAL

Draw three circles on a blank piece of paper or in your journal and name them threat, drive and soothe. Write in the appropriate circle the brief answers to the following questions. You can then expand your thinking further by journalling on each question.

- What triggers your own systems of threat, drive and soothe?
- How much time do you spend in each of these systems?
- What can you introduce to work towards a better balance between the systems?

How the model gave me clarity

I noticed this model explained the stages that I went through during my breakup. The emotional systems can be used to give you an insight into where you are emotionally and what system you are operating from when you are upset.

When my husband left, it felt like a huge threat to my safety and to the safety of my family. I was worried about maintaining a home, and where the money would come from to pay the bills. I was anxious about my children's well-being and emotional states. I was angry at being put in the situation I faced.

My confidence took a huge knock and I felt extremely vulnerable. Things that seemed so easy before were quite terrifying now. There was also a level of shame and anxiety about what other people would think of me and the situation. I felt threatened by embarrassment. At first when people asked where he was, I said he was away for work, not wanting to deal with or face questions that I didn't even know the answers to.

Then the drive system kicked in. My wonderful family and friends encouraged me to stop thinking about him and start thinking about me. To put down focusing on how to repair my relationship and to get my ship in order. To consider the resources that I needed and to decide on a plan of action. They reminded me that I needed some solid ground underneath my feet before I could move forward with anything else. That looking after myself and my children's welfare were my priorities.

The drive system gave me the fuel I needed to face some very uncomfortable and, to me, mortifying activities such as seeking government help. I had many difficult yet important conversations that took up hours and hours. I spoke to my mortgage company, creditors, the bank, utility companies, and local council services just to name a few.

I sobbed on the phone to the Citizens Advice Bureau, who were absolutely amazing. They managed to manoeuvre my ship off the rocks and into safer waters. They offered help and support in a myriad of different ways. I was so touched by their kindness and extremely thankful for all the services available to me.

The drive system propelled me to look for a suitable job so that I could be available for the kids, whilst at the same time keeping a roof over our heads and food on the table. My emotional state included determination, bravery and grit, which helped me to work through the toughest days and get into a position where I was out of survival and on my way to thriving.

Once my system recognised that the kids and I were safe and had the resources, tools and support in good order, then I was able to rebuild. I could access more readily the soothe emotional system and I could begin to see how I could be content again.

I was soothed by the simple things like having plenty of toilet roll, fat balls in the bird feeder, and petrol in my car. These became my measuring sticks of contentment and of doing OK. Then my measuring sticks transitioned to feeling more settled in my job, Molly managing more days at college, and Oliver passing his driving test. Eventually, this led to me feeling content watching TV alone at night, talking openly to friends and confidently planning out future activities.

I, like you, always had access to my soothing system, however it took much more effort to be mindful to go there during the days of heightened stress. An effort definitely worth making.

Chapter 11

YOUR CORE NEEDS

Most of us were never taught what we need in order to feel safe, secure and loved.

When you have experienced safety, security and love, you know that you are worthy of it. And you also know what to look out for. You naturally gravitate towards people who offer it and you swiftly change course when you come across the people who don't.

But if these basic needs were not fulfilled in your early life, this inner knowing might not come so naturally. You may have a sense that something's missing and feel frustrated and hurt, but you probably won't know what to do about it. You might even struggle to put your finger on what the issue is.

The problem with this is that it leaves you passive, allowing life — and people — to lead you in all kinds of directions, whether they suit you or not.

When you don't know what you need, how can you expect other people to know what you need?

Your relationship with yourself comes first and foremost. As soon as you've identified your needs, you empower yourself with the ability to ask for them to be met. Of course, that doesn't mean that they will be. But hopefully it means that you'll get most of them met.

LOOKING THROUGH THE NINE STAR KI LENS

How do you know then, which emotional needs to look out for? Being able to identify which emotional need is unmet can give you a rough idea of what you can start working on. Knowing what the core emotional needs are can be a good starting point to understanding your persistent pain points such as feeling like your life is lacking something or is empty; common feelings when you aren't fulfilled from within.

I will introduce you to a few ways that can assist you with this including utilising your Nine Star Ki inner/ heart number.

Let's begin by looking at each of the five elements: water, earth, wood, metal and fire. I will share each of the elements' core needs and drivers and which emotions indicate imbalance.

Your inner/ heart number is the energy of your inner landscape, the seat of your emotions and can give you lots of information about how to self-regulate and self-soothe, and what to look for as indicators of being stressed and out of balance.

You can think of the emotional driver as similar to Gilbert's drive system.

Refer to your Nine Star Ki numbers as illustrated in the chart and look at what element your inner number is. For example, 1 is Water, 2,5,8, are Earth, 3,4 are Wood/ Tree, 6,7 are Metal and 9 is Fire.

ELEMENTS — CORE NEEDS

Core needs are the feelings and tasks that each element thrives on, incorporating them into your life as much as possible enables you to feel aligned, purposeful and content.

Start with focusing on your inner number, then add the other elemental needs associated with all three of your Nine Star Ki and eventually ensure all five are met.

For example, my Nine Star Ki is 4.1.8, 1 Water being my inner/ heart number. I benefit from focusing on self-discipline like going to the gym regularly, whilst being mindful of constricting my behaviour because I fear the consequences — like letting my hair down and dancing without fear of ridicule. I also check in with how I am nourishing myself and others, and what I am doing to learn and grow whilst maintain healthy boundaries.

- **Fire** needs to feel joy, to be spontaneous and play without feeling guilty or having to 'deserve it', and to receive warmth and love.

- **Water** needs to be able to assess risk and realistic limits. To have sufficient self-control and discipline to complete necessary tasks, without excessively following rules or fearing the consequences of doing so.

- **Earth** needs to nourish others and be nourished, to be cared about unconditionally and supported. Needs a sense of stability, safety and acceptance by a caregiver or loved one.

- **Wood** needs to learn and grow; to be assertive and have good boundaries. Must be allowed to make independent decisions, complete tasks, and to take appropriate responsibility for them.

- **Metal** needs to be able to process loss and grief and express emotions without being punished or invalidated. Also needs acknowledgement and recognition for their achievements.

When you know what you fundamentally need to be in a balanced state of body, mind and spirit then you can work towards cultivating more of that energy in your life. When you know what to look for, you are able to recognise it when it appears. You can confidently ask for your specific needs to be met because you know it benefits your well-being.

Being aware of how you feel and what your natural state is when in balance is very useful, you can use the emotions and thoughts you experience as a guide, like a litmus test. When you then find yourself out of balance it is easier to spot and remedy.

Prolonged periods of stress are detrimental to your health and so whilst it is normal to have times of stress and imbalance it is best not to stay stuck there. Being out of balance can cause confusion and anxiety, conflicts in your relationships, and a lack of drive and purpose; perhaps leading to issues at work and physical symptoms such as headaches and stomach upsets.

Emotions of elements out of balance

- **Fire:** Lack of joy or sadness
- **Water:** Fear and abandonment issues
- **Earth:** Sympathy and worry
- **Wood:** Anger or frustration
- **Metal:** Grief or loss.

Signs of imbalance can start off subtly and then get louder and more intense until you address them. Your thoughts and experiences are a good measure of whether you are moving out of balance.

Each element has clues to imbalance, so if you start to experience these warning signs or questions coming to mind it's time to pause and take stock.

Here are the challenging aspects of each stage and some of the remedies to help rebalance them.

- **Water:** Fear, lack of trust and loneliness. **Remedy** is to do nothing, float, relax.
- **Wood:** Anger, feeling blocked and misunderstandings. **Remedy** is to define your goals and act.
- **Fire:** Lack of joy, heartbreak and feeling rejected. **Remedy** is to explore what makes your heart sing.
- **Earth:** Worry, weak boundaries and a lack of support. **Remedy** is to look at what needs to be organised or completed and ask for help.
- **Metal:** Anxiety, grief and lack of self-esteem. **Remedy** is breathwork, letting go and predictability.

Let's get more specific and look at what nourishes and regulates each of the nine archetypes' emotions

Nine Star Ki Inner Numbers are nourished by:

- **1 Water:** Silence, being and allowing time for thinking or feeling deeply, together with a sense of freedom beyond fear.
- **2 Earth:** A sense of connection, gathering friends and family together, sharing food and catching up with each other.

- **3 Tree**: Encouragement to pursue your ambitions with the steady support and love of others, balancing independence with connection to fuel your growth.
- **4 Tree**: Talking and sound, writing and other creative and artistic ways of expression.
- **5 Earth**: Receiving positive attention such as encouragement or being acknowledged, helping you to shine.
- **6 Metal**: A core values system to follow, minimalist - clear and tidy - space, quality in terms of both items and time, truthfulness.
- **7 Metal**: Harmony and the ability to reflect on what they do and don't like, to exercise and experience touch like massage or hugs.
- **8 Earth**: Books, libraries and mysteries, research and history. Looking back to bring things into the present. Daydreaming, contemplation, health and the human body.
- **9 Fire**: Being centre stage, having a range of fun activities to do and spreading love through being a good friend or making people laugh.

It's reassuring to be mindful of how your emotional needs dance with each other, as when they pop up you can recognise them and will not be so easily fazed by them.

For example Molly, whose Nine Star Ki is 4.3.6, had a discombobulating experience with her college tutor, whom she admired and felt comfortable with normally. This day her tutor had a lot on her mind and was not her usual self. Molly picked up on her tutor's change in energy as she is sensitive and empathic, and found it disconcerting and confusing. Molly took it to heart and didn't feel like she could talk to her tutor as freely as usual.

Feeling unable to express her thoughts, and therefore missing out on receiving reassurance and recognition, did not meet Molly's emotional needs and so she felt somewhat bereft. It subtly reminded her of the feelings of grief she had around her dad leaving the family home and not receiving the answers and reassurance she needed from him.

When Molly realised that she was taking on her tutor's energy unnecessarily and was inadvertently allowing it to trigger her, she could release that burden and felt a lot better. She remembered a saying: "Not your monkeys, not your circus", which made her laugh and in turn shifted her emotions back to a more positive, balanced state.

Emotional intelligence

In 1995 Daniel Goleman published the groundbreaking book, "Emotional Intelligence", and shone a spotlight on the importance and power of emotions. Through his research he was able to show that your success in life is based as much, if not more, on your ability to manage your emotions than your intellectual capabilities. He defines Emotional Intelligence as consisting of five skills: knowing your emotions, managing emotions, motivating yourself, recognising emotions in others and handling relationships.

From his work, a new field of psychology was born called Positive Psychology, which discovered that positive emotional states broaden your thinking. Negative emotions, on the other hand, can prevent you from reaching the states you need to access problem-solving and creativity.

Generating feelings of appreciation, love, care and compassion, enables you to experience a deeper level of intuition and insight for more effective decisions in day-to-day life. Positive emotions like love, appreciation, care and compassion help to balance your nervous system.

Without experiencing the wisdom of listening to your heart and enhancing your emotional intelligence, your mind is more susceptible to reactive emotions such as anger, fear, insecurity and blame.

You can learn to recognise emotions and attitudes that drain you and replace them with more positive ones that provide enlightened perspectives.

The mind rationalises — it can make you think that you are justified in being angry.

The heart is softer, it whispers to you with quiet common sense.

It takes courage to listen to your heart.

The key is to use emotion in a balanced way. To listen to what your feeling is telling you and then work out how to act upon it in a way that is beneficial for the situation, your life and the world around you.

It may be though that even before you learn to recognise your emotions, a reminder is in order; a reminder for you to truly know that it is worth the effort, that you are awesome. That you are more than brilliant; you are loved unconditionally simply for being you and exactly as you are. I potentially need to remind you that your light may currently be dimmed, that does not mean it has been lost. It is there, hidden under layers of fears, doubts, blame, shame and untrue stories that you have believed for so long.

Sometimes there is a necessity to let life crack you open to reveal your power and beauty within.

THE REASON FOR MISTRUST IN YOURSELF

The negative bias and your "tinker brain"

Your human brain is amazing, and its primary job is to keep you alive. The aim of keeping you safe and out of danger is paramount. Whilst humans have evolved and developed the capacity to think about things, to ruminate, worry and consider, the brain has not evolved to maintain a healthy or positive mindset. Instead, you have a "threat mindset" that is hard-wired, otherwise known as the negativity bias which fixes and focuses on what can go wrong.

Rick Hanson, PhD describes the negativity bias as: "We're velcro for difficult experiences and teflon for pleasant ones."

This means that you often receive messages that say: "*What can go wrong?*" Your brain defaults to looking for negativity so that you remain cautious and therefore safe. But, if left unchecked in times of stress, the message "What can go wrong?" turns into "What's wrong with me?" which becomes personalised. If you do not have a solid base of self-love, this negative bias can feed mistrust, thoughts and beliefs. It can be easy to forget how wonderful you are and cover the truth of who you are in thoughts and feelings around unworthiness.

I like to compassionately and playfully call this part of my brain "tinker". A tinker to me is up to mischief and is not being malicious. Catching your negative thoughts in this way and remembering "that's my tinker brain" can diffuse a negative thought thread quickly and painlessly. Instead of being judgemental or resisting your brain's natural ways, you can be kind.

Your tinker brain can be very subtle and get your mind tangled like spaghetti very easily. The trick is to catch yourself in the act. If you don't catch yourself in the moment, it is still useful to catch yourself as soon as you can to bring yourself back to feeling good or neutral again.

Here's an example for you.

> I was driving over to my mum's for dinner and needed some petrol. I stopped at the nearest petrol station, pulled up to the pump, shut the door and locked the car. I then attempted to open the petrol cap, but it was jammed shut. My first thought was it was air-locked and maybe needed a bit of extra strength, so I asked the gentleman in the car in front for some assistance. He pulled it, jiggled it and gave it a shake to no avail. He suggested getting some help from a garage the following morning and to now go and enjoy my dinner.
>
> My petrol light was flashing but he assured me I'd have enough petrol, saying it was amazing how many miles I would get out of it. I left the petrol station and thoughts started whirring away.
>
> "I don't have RAC anymore, perhaps if I call them and re-join, they can come and sort it at Mum's? But I don't really want that extra cover or expense now. And maybe it wouldn't be covered straight away.."
>
> More thoughts consumed my mind, and I felt worried.
>
> "It's Sunday tomorrow and garages will be shut, what if I need something from the shop, what if...?"
>
> I got to Mum's house and explained my problem. She considered it for a moment and then asked: "So you locked the car?" She went on "Do you usually lock it before getting petrol? Did you try and unlock the car and then open the petrol cap?"
>
> I laughed and said: "Oh if it's that simple, then great!" I went back to my car, unlocked it and lo and behold the petrol cap opened with ease.
>
> When I locked the car, as a safety feature it stopped me from opening the petrol cap to put fuel in it. Just like your brain's safety feature is to lock

out the positives and focus on the negatives, my car was keeping me safe. Safe from losing petrol. Once I recognised this, I was immediately able to fill my tank back up for many more journeys.

One of my favourite stories to illustrate how your light and your gifts can be hidden is the Golden Buddha.

THE GOLDEN BUDDHA

Many years ago, in Thailand was a temple with a huge golden Buddha. One day the villagers got word that the Burmese army was about to invade, so they helped the monks cover the golden Buddha, made of solid gold and very valuable, with clay so it looked plain, and the invading army would perceive no value in it.

The army moved through the village and temple and passed by the earthen Buddha with no reason to steal it. For many years, the army occupied the village with this temple and Buddha. With time there was no longer anyone who remembered that the Buddha was golden.

Then one day in 1957, a young monk was meditating at the base of the Buddha when a glint of something shining from a small crack in the Buddha caught his eye. The monk excitedly told the other monks, and they used a hammer and chisel to chip away at the clay covering until he revealed the statue was a golden Buddha.

Over the course of your life, your golden Buddha, which is a metaphor here for your purpose and light, gets covered in layer upon layer of clay. The heaviest layers are your own limiting self-beliefs that prevent you from following your dreams, living life in alignment with your true self, and fulfilling your potential.

The other layers of clay are added by external conditioning from parents and caregivers, schools and teachers, bosses and co-workers, society and the media. Eventually you are so laden with clay that you forget that the golden Buddha is always there within you.

The secret to finding your golden Buddha — your higher purpose or golden nature — lies in your deepest wounds and cracks. Something occurs in your life such as a loss, major change or tragedy that breaks you open, enough to see the gold within. And so, you start chipping away at the clay to rediscover your true self, to unveil more of the golden you, where your peace and contentment reside.

You can then reconnect with what makes your heart sing, what you value most and what motivates you to get out of bed with a smile on your face. Your curiosity rises along with the excitement about the new opportunities ahead of you, enabling you to discover things that propel you towards your new life and goals. The more you chip away the old unhealthy habits and limiting beliefs, the more gold you will find.

THE POWER OF SELF-REGULATION

When you have sovereignty over your emotions, you can harness your own power, and stand strong, grounded in your values and convictions. To have the ability to stick up for yourself when needed even if it's scary.

There seems to be a tipping point between staying small and quiet or resentful, angry and lonely and feeling the fear and doing it anyway. Or to put it another way, reaching a turning point where self-love and self-compassion become non-negotiables for you. You may not realise you have reached this point until something happens and you approach it in a new way.

I was proud of myself in the moments I became aware that my heart wasn't beating as hard, that I felt calmer and less fuzzy-headed. When I opened an email or had to deal with a challenging conversation and felt in control rather than wanting to escape or hide. When I realised that I was doing too much for other people and started to say no before handing the reigns of responsibility back to them.

I had tipped over into an inner sense of strength and determination. Not necessarily a loud roar, more like a rising sense of assurity and contentment.

How you approach this is very much influenced by your personal energy pattern.

For example, a 1 Water heart number will influence your emotions and the way you respond to situations in specific ways. The way your 1 Water energy dances with your birth and soul numbers will then nuance this.

Being aware of your unique pattern and becoming familiar with it through observing how you approach situations, will help you to access a balanced approach. To respond rather than react.

Remember that reacting means you have effectively lost your inner balance. This tends to lead to impulsive outbursts, ill-thought-out actions, and feelings of shame or guilt once you have regained your composure. This in turn can erode your self-confidence and feed self-doubt.

When you have a strong reaction to something that in reality is small, benign or not appropriate to the level of your reaction, it is likely to stem from an echo of the past. Noticing, for example, that you are experiencing a strong emotion to someone leaving a cup in the sink or using the last bit of toilet roll and not replacing it, could be a step towards healing. It alerts you to a deeper hurt underneath.

Once you have identified you are experiencing suffering, for example, that you feel hurt, angry, used, or invisible, then you can self-inquire as to the root of that feeling. The antidote to being overwhelmed with strong emotional reactions is to practice identifying your feelings as they happen, until you notice that a tipping point has occurred. Something that tips you over into negative feelings like frustration. Once you get the hang of noticing your emotions and feelings as they are happening, then it's a case of maintenance, which is a lifelong endeavour.

Let's take Paul as a case study, his Nine Star Ki is 5.1.9

As a child, Paul often felt like an outsider, alone and overlooked. His way of coping with this was to bottle up his deeply held emotions and to withdraw. He came to believe that he was defective due to the way he was treated.

Over time, he began to realise that he was not defective and in fact he had been mistreated. He studied Psychology at university and gained a degree which helped him to understand why people behave in the ways they do. The veil of illusion slipped more and more until he began to realise that he was OK, and he did not have to tolerate the abuse. This realisation allowed his emotions to surface.

Paul's soul number is 9 Fire, a passionate warm and loving energy. His soul was so fired up one day about the injustice around a conversation he had with a family member that it began to heat up and 'boil' his inner 1 Water — his inner emotions.

Imagine, if you will, Paul's inner emotions as a pan of water over a flame. Eventually the water will boil and cause the lid to come off the pan, producing a lot of steam. The conversation made Paul so angry that he felt his mounting anger could lead to a heart attack. He was shocked by the force of his emotions boiling over, this came as a wake-up call.

Paul then began to practice feeling his emotions rising and before they got to boiling point to release the pent-up energy in a more controlled manner. He did this in a variety of ways including using exercise, space clearing and journalling.

My emotional journey

My Nine Star Ki is 4.1.8 and although I, like Paul, have 1 Water as an inner/heart number, I experience and heal my emotional responses in ways that are unique to me. My birth and soul numbers also distinguish how I perceive and work through challenging situations.

I grew up with an authoritarian, practical-minded mother and an easy-going father. Being a quiet and gentle person, I was easily influenced by my more dominant mother and I became a typical 'good girl'. As my father modelled keeping the peace, I learnt to be compliant and not to express my needs or stand up for myself.

I would experience a visceral fear within when I wanted to do something outside of what I thought was expected of me. This deep fear would often stop me in my tracks and prevent me from going ahead due to being frozen in fear.

On the other side of fear is love. The more that I learnt to love and accept myself the more I was able to confidently move forward with my vision and plans. I am supported by my strong and nurturing 8 Earth energy. A symbol for 8 Earth is the Mountain and inside this mountain is a cave. This cave is where I can go to access my soul's wisdom. I can also imagine standing tall and firm like a majestic mountain.

The tipping point for me was my separation and the mix of feelings that were brought up because of it. Until then I had allowed my emotions to be let out in measured and careful ways, often in a trickle. After my break-up, I learnt to allow my emotions to flow. Then as I gained in confidence, I was able to articulate and express them clearly.

Paul and I's 1 Water heart energy causes us to experience deep feelings, like a well that you can't see the bottom of. We both experienced the fear of the unknown like peering into deep dark water and not wanting to jump in. Yet we both summoned the strength of 1 Water, which is courage, to work through our fears and utilise their wisdom.

Healing the wounds of your childhood or inner child can bring such freedom and empowerment. A happy contented inner child, just like any child tends to be more creative, have more fun and have the freedom to explore their own interests and ideas.

I have found it immensely useful to be aware of my wounds and how they manifest in my daily life, and I hope seeing your inner child through the lens of Nine Star Ki will help you too.

Emotional awareness and self-regulation

Emotional awareness involves being conscious of what you are feeling and the ability to observe your responses and behaviours. To gain a better understanding of your emotions, an important to skill to cultivate is tuning into your internal body signals. If you were not encouraged to listen to your body in childhood, haven't taken the time to focus on what may be going on in your body or are neurodiverse, this may be new to you.

Butterflies in your stomach, a racing heart, tense muscles, or a distracted brain can provide very important clues to your emotions. Becoming more aware of exactly how your body is feeling will ultimately help you gain a better understanding of your emotions. And this will lead to the ability to self-regulate your emotions in a more successful way.

To understand the emotions involved in any given situation without them taking over you is the essence of self-regulation. Asking yourself "How am I feeling?" and becoming aware of how you feel and why is reassuring and empowering.

Your body doesn't lie

Being aware of your body's cues and your default reaction when something causes an emotional disturbance within you is extremely useful and very powerful. Having the ability to identify when you are going into a default reaction or have been triggered can help you to skilfully navigate difficult feelings and interactions.

It takes intention, mindfulness and practice to catch yourself in the moment and have the tools to proactively respond instead of reacting.

Victor Frankl, an Austrian psychotherapist, was a master at this. He wrote the autobiographical "Man's Search for Meaning" after surviving the horrors of the holocaust in Nazi concentration camps. He wrote:

"Between stimulus and response there is a space. In that space is our power to choose our response. In our response lies our growth and our freedom."

There are several things that you need to be aware of to fully appreciate the skill involved in the seemingly simple task that Victor Frankl refers to.

Firstly, you need to allow yourself the space. To give yourself full permission to come out of the shadows and stand in your truth and power. You may be very used to making yourself small, shrinking and not taking up much space. Allowing worrying or negative thoughts to fill your mind prevents the space for new and empowering thoughts to emerge. Perhaps you have told yourself that you are content helping other people feel happy. That their happiness is enough for you and therefore you have a habit of expressing few of your needs.

Now however, hiding, not getting your needs met and having your feelings discounted is growing thin. You may be beginning to feel ignored, stepped on and even taken advantage of.

Once this feeling of impending, empowering change starts rising within you, it will not be contained. Once you accept that you deserve more, the cat is out of the bag and will not go back in. Rightly so.

Once you recognise that there is a space you can move into and take up, the second step is to recognise your default reactions. A reaction is different to a response.

A reaction happens quickly, often without thought or awareness and can cause you to be impulsive; to say and do things you may later regret or feel guilty about. A response is measured, thought out and felt through and is intentional.

TAKE FIVE PAUSE AND PRACTICE

Tune into your body

Recognising your default reactions

When something bothers you, what happens in your body and mind?

Perhaps someone says something or behaves in a way that causes you discomfort. Can you take a moment to explore what goes on inside your body? What sensations do you notice?

Take some deep relaxing breaths, settle into a comfortable and upright posture and bring to mind an interaction or conversation that is causing or has caused you anxiety, anger or anguish.

Scan your body from the tips of your toes to the top of your head and allow yourself to feel the sensations arising. Where do you notice the change in your body?

Is there tightness in your chest?

Do you feel sick?

Perhaps a squirmy sensation or butterflies in your stomach?

Heat rising to your cheeks?

A lump in your throat?

Being aware of what happens in your body when under stress, enables you to practice catching yourself as it happens. This takes a little time and effort and is worth it. Having the cues before you react is very helpful in avoiding uttering words or taking actions that you may later regret when you are back in equilibrium.

You are a work in progress, as are all of us and so it's important to remember to be kind to yourself. You are a human being and as so will make mistakes and say and do things that in hindsight you would have done differently. The trick is to have some compassion for yourself and know that you can always begin again. Every moment is a new moment to be embraced.

Chapter 12

COMPASSION

Compassion is one of the highest forms of human emotion. It is what connects you to others. Compassion embodies a tangible expression of love, like a big warm hug. The feeling of being safe in moments of distress or the experience of profound relief that follows experiencing a deep level of caring. Compassion involves a desire to alleviate suffering and is one of the most valuable skills within emotional regulation you can learn for yourself.

The meaning of compassion is to recognise the suffering of others and then take action to help. There are two types of compassion: the compassion you have for others and the compassion you have for yourself which is self-compassion.

As a society compassion is often shown for others and yet it isn't widely encouraged to be compassionate towards yourself, leaving many people starved of emotional connection and support. Self-compassion is vital in times of stress and suffering. It is also the best defence against one-sided, toxic and unhealthy relationships. When you have self-compassion, gaslighting, negative behaviour and being demeaned will not be tolerated. It's like kryptonite for negative energy.

The power of self-compassion

So why is it so powerful?

Building self-compassion evolves resilience, it strengthens your resolve. It enables you to cultivate an inner strength that is warm, kind and considerate. You begin to care more about yourself and your boundaries. Instead of thinking about the welfare of other people first, you can consider yourself. This is not selfish; it is self-preservation which is your absolute right.

Self-compassion is a superpower, and it is within your power to learn it. Practice using this skill to create a happier, calmer and contented mind. Self-compassion is not simple, if it was then knowing what it is would be enough.

Self-compassion is being able to recognise when you are suffering and accept it. Once you have accepted it then you can use practices and tools to alleviate your suffering. As the saying goes pain is inevitable, suffering is optional.

You can acknowledge you are suffering and that you have the power to do something about it by saying out loud or in your mind the self-compassion mantra.

Self-compassion mantra

This is hard and I'm OK.

I've got this.

This mantra helps to ground you in the present moment. It helps you to recognise that you are anxious, worried or distressed and suffering. Once you have conscious awareness then you can take action steps.

Remember your tinker brain? It's useful to remind yourself of how it works when you get caught up in self-criticism, doubt or shame. It is not your fault that you think this way. There is a part of your brain called the amygdala that works to protect you and is resistant to change. Whenever you attempt to change a habit or thinking pattern that involves a new goal or direction, the change will automatically be resisted. Knowing this can help you to strengthen your resolve and persevere with being kind to yourself.

Building self-compassion is like building a muscle, you need to give it regular exercise to become stronger. If you don't use the muscle, it will weaken and not work as well.

Mindfulness and meditation are the foundational practices to build self-compassion. They help you to practice slowing down and catching yourself in moments of suffering. This enables you to stand back and observe your thoughts and feelings. Then intentionally redirect or refocus your attention onto more self-compassionate thoughts and ideas. I would wholeheartedly recommend practising mindfulness daily, five minutes a day can elevate your well-being.

TAKE FIVE PAUSE AND JOURNAL

When genuinely feeling compassionate you naturally display a soft attentive half-smile, a calm, shoulders-back, head-up stance whilst offering a caring touch and a warm gentle tone of voice.

I invite you to deliberately adopt a compassionate facial expression, body posture and tone of voice and whilst in this compassionate state, journal on the following sentence stems:

- Being self-compassionate towards myself looks like...
- The advice I would give to a friend I deeply care about who was thinking and feeling this way is...
- The compassionate part of me would say..........to the self-critical part

These journal prompts give a voice to the compassionate side of you, A voice that you may not have heard for a long time, which brings new balanced perspectives about the true importance of a situation.

Compassionate connection

Connection is *"the energy that exists between people when they feel seen, heard, valued; when they can give and receive without judgement; and when they derive sustenance and strength from the relationship."*

- Brene Brown

Sharing something very personal with another and revealing what you have been through, sets off a chemical reaction in their mind and body, which creates a connection. It may be quite alien to you to reach out for help when you are upset, especially if you have been discouraged to do so in the past.

Reassuringly, reaching out to trusted friends and family members benefits you both. Instead of feeling like you are bothering someone or are burdensome

— which is not true, I hasten to add — that you get the support you need to lift a weight off your shoulders. The other person has the gift of being of service and help which feels good. Plus, you build stronger connections and relationships by learning more about each other.

TAKE FIVE PAUSE AND ACTION

Compassionate truth game

Find a partner and a pack of playing cards

The aim of this game is to gently build your confidence around speaking your truth. To say what's on your mind in a safe, encouraging and reciprocal way. It has three levels that get progressively more challenging.

Each level is indicated by the number of cards put down, so your partner is aware of what level of sharing you have decided upon. Whilst there is no expectation to go up to a level three until you feel comfortable enough to do so, it is worthwhile to attempt it.

The benefit of the game is to show you that sharing your innermost thoughts can bring you relief, and build confidence, self-esteem and connection.

How to Play

Decide on who will go first and then you will each take turns to share.

Consider scenarios, worries or concerns that you would like to bring out into the open. Perhaps a decision you are mulling over or something you have been keeping hidden due to fear of embarrassment or shame.

Decide the level of vulnerability it takes to share this and place the appropriate number of cards in front of your partner.

There are 3 levels to this exercise; easy, medium, hard or sheepish, embarrassed and fearful.

One card represents something that you feel slightly nervous sharing.

Two cards represent something that you feel sheepish saying out loud.

Three cards represent something much bigger and deeply personal.

Begin by stating how many cards you have put down and then share your thoughts.

When you have finished your partner will reply with a simple statement of *"Thank you for sharing"*.

If they would like clarification or to check they have heard everything you wanted to share correctly, they can ask if it's OK to reflect back to you what they understood. Reflection is useful for you as the sharer as it may bring new ideas to mind.

Continue to take turns sharing until you feel complete, or your designated amount of time has elapsed.

The inner critic

"You are your own worst critic", the old saying goes. It is true that most people are hard on themselves, you and I included.

There is a critical voice in your head that points out your flaws and mistakes, everyone has one to some degree. This voice is also known as the ego, It's the part of you that is working against you. It is not bad, just intense. The inner critic or ego is the voice within that gives you the choice in every moment whether to choose love or not.

Your inner critic can come out in full force when you are experiencing change, loss or pain. It's that berating voice that shouts in your head when you have the smallest hint of not measuring up in some way. The ego uses time against you, it's the energy of "If you don't do this immediately something bad will happen to you." It also makes false promises like: "If you do this, you're going to be rich".

The voice that says:

"You should have done this."

"What a stupid mistake to make."

"You have failed, let down, caused an issue..."

Often your inner critic goes undetected and abuses you under the radar, without conscious awareness. Once you catch yourself saying things that you wouldn't dream of saying to other people, then you can do something about how you speak to yourself. Awareness is key.

I watched as her frustration mounted.

"Come here, come HERE and look at this", she said impatiently, as he continued to play, not paying any attention to what she was saying.

"Come here and look at this picture or I'll tell Daddy you've been naughty and there's no party." His head swiftly turned to look at his grandma and reluctantly popped himself up onto the sofa to look at the picture she was so adamant he must see.

No sooner had he continued with his own fun, she bellowed again: "Get up off the floor, stop doing that, come here and sit still."

This grandma was clearly feeling out of control of her little grandson who was waiting eagerly to go into his own fifth birthday party. Whilst it's easy to have an opinion about her parenting strategy, watching her was like a reflection of what had been happening in my world the last few days.

My frustration, stemming from fear, had been escalating. Fuelled by a myriad of bombarding thoughts around moving house. A barrage of self-abuse mixed with excitement going on in my head.

"If it's not clean and tidy, they will think I'm a slob."

"If it's not all nicely decorated, they won't see the value and won't want to buy it, then I won't have the money to..."

I don't know what was going on in the grandma's head however I can take a bet that she had some self-deprecation going on around being judged in some way.

My feelings of frustration, helplessness and resistance to what was occurring spilled out at home as the kids made excuses, moans and groans about tidying their rooms and getting the house prepared for viewings.

A volcano building inside me, heat bubbling away, simmering and occasionally erupting. Thoughts like, "Why won't they just help? I help them so much and when I need it most, they aren't there for me." My mind grasping for ways to make them see, to do what I wanted them to do. Panic at the thought of people coming and the house reflecting badly on me.

Then it dawned on me that they were having a different experience around moving than I was. It was the only home they had ever known, their safe haven and sanctuary. Whilst my focus was on a clean slate, a new start and something fresh, their grieving had morphed from losing their dad to losing their home.

It wasn't that they didn't want to help me, it was they didn't want to move. It was another choice that they did not make. I had confused stubbornness for insubordination and reacted. Once I realised what was going on, I softened. Instead of beating myself up about reacting, I had compassion for myself. It's OK to have times when things are a bit much, when circumstances and feelings are overwhelming. It's an opportunity to learn, grow and begin again.

The main thing I had to give myself compassion for was the use of threats. In my triggered whirlwind of a mind, I felt completely out of control, tossed around and flung up in the air with swirling thoughts. I grasped onto what had been modelled to me. A small voice whispering it was not the best way to approach it and yet the words still flew out of my mouth.

"If you don't help me, don't expect me to help you again with x,y,z".

"If you don't help me, I'll find a two-bedroom house instead of three."

Of course, shouting and threats didn't work. They dug their heels in even more and what was worse, they were now hurt and upset. I took a step back and reached for a better way for all of us. I sat them down and told them the reasons it was important to me for the house to be in a good state. I pointed out the positives of moving and described the bigger picture. I encouraged them by suggesting ways that they could get involved in the process.

After I had some buy-in and a slither of enthusiasm, things changed and they helped with a simple ask. They would come to me with phones in hand showing me pictures of the houses they had been looking at and the desired accessories for their new rooms. Peace reigned in the house now that we were all on the same side again.

When you want someone to do something and they are resistant, it can feel very uncomfortable. The trick is to pause, take a step back and be curious about the resistance. An inner ease creates a receptive space for intuitive ideas and feelings to emerge.

Ask yourself, what is this experience or situation showing you? Bring in some love and compassion for yourself and for them. Remember that you care for this person and attempt to view it from their perspective. How is their experience different from yours? How can you meet in the middle?

Shouting only leads to more shouting.

Meet it with calm reasoning and coaxing.

Resistance leads to impatience and resentment.

Meet it with compassion, gentleness and the bigger picture.

If you feel your frustration rising, take a break, breathe and check in on your thoughts. Ensure that you are not being inadvertently driven by negative thoughts and feelings. Take hold of the wheel and get back into the driving seat of your life. Speak directly to the energy. Navigate through the resistance by letting it know your truth.

For example, say out loud or inside your head what you are experiencing.

"Argh I feel you, frustration. I feel helpless and at the same time anger building up inside. I feel shaky, out of control. It's not nice feeling like this. I want to feel calmer. I don't know what's come over me. I'd like to figure this out."

Resistance occurs when there is a part of you that feels like it does not deserve the positive shift or change. When in truth, you do deserve all good things. Choose to accept this shift, this change wholeheartedly.

Emotions and regaining power

If your emotions are not acknowledged, expressed or validated, they tend to be buried, stuffed down or swallowed. That doesn't mean that they disappear, instead they swirl around in your body and can make you feel sad, nervous or frustrated. Suppressed emotions often spurt out as irritability which can hurt other people, particularly those closest to you.

If in your childhood or past experiences, you have been discouraged from sharing your feelings or have been shamed for having them, you have most likely learnt to have little tolerance for them. If you missed the emotional training, you were ideally meant to learn as a child, then it is likely that you don't have easy access to your emotions. Feelings themselves are not bad or wrong. You cannot choose your feelings. You can choose to connect with them and find out what they are pointing to so that you can respond instead of reacting.

Being in touch with your emotions and feelings gives you more energy, direction and motivation. As you realise that you are not damaged or inadequate in any way, you can start to feel good about yourself. You understand that you are just as valid and important as everyone else. Feeling good about yourself then enables you to stop making yourself small by shrinking and hiding and to take up more space.

Taking up more space can mean making your presence known by speaking up for yourself, being honest and acting. It feels completely different in your body and mind to allow yourself to fully expand and open.

TAKE FIVE PAUSE AND PRACTICE

Star power pose

This exercise is a great one for truly experiencing taking up more space and the positive effect it can have on your confidence and self-worth.

Take a seat and bring to mind a thought that causes you frustration or sadness for a moment. Then, cross your arms and legs and allow your forehead to drop down slowly towards your knees, fold your body forward and tuck your chin to your chest.

In this scrunched-up position notice what happens to your thoughts and feelings.

Now unfurl yourself slowly, release your legs so that your feet are firmly placed on the floor, uncross your arms and gently raise your head.

Notice how that posture changes your state — the way your body feels and the quality of your thoughts.

Now I invite you to stand up. Place your feet hip-width apart, lift your head and look up to the sky. Raise your arms and stretch your hands up to the sky. You are now in a star shape. Turn your lips into a smile and feel the strength, power and space you have created.

Have a go now at thinking about the negative thought from earlier.

You will notice that it is much harder to access.

TAKE FIVE PAUSE AND ACTION

In the times when you notice a feeling of dread or apprehension wash over you. Pause and tune inwards. Ask yourself: "What am I hiding from?" "Am I concealing something?" "Where am I shrinking instead of standing in my power?"

I invite you to stop hiding the real you.

Claim yourself, claim your power, claim your worth.

Inward and outward focus

Focusing excessively on the outside world takes you away from what really matters: YOU.

When you have a habit of wondering what other people are doing, thinking and feeling instead of focusing inward on what you want, believe and feel, then you are giving your power away.

If your emotions were consistently invalidated as a child, you likely developed a pattern of giving away your power. It was your way of ensuring that you received love and care. Being told things like: *"Don't cry or I'll give you something to cry about"*, *"You don't want that"*, and *"You don't need that"* set you up for learning not to trust your choices and feelings. Your decisions were overruled and your power was given to someone else.

When you are used to looking outwards, seeking validation and answers from others, it makes it difficult for you to make your own decisions. Trusting yourself to make the right decisions for you takes practice. You can start with small things like asking yourself if you'd prefer tea or coffee and work up to bigger decisions as you build in confidence. Please be gentle with yourself as you practice, you are learning. We are all a work in progress.

Identifying your values, needs and boundaries are wonderful ways to deepen your relationship with yourself and others. The more you can connect with and express who you are and what you want, the easier it becomes to ask for what you need. Sharing your feelings cuts through the facts and details and gets straight to the heart of what matters. It opens doors and pulls down walls.

Remember to choose you.

Take back your power

It is easier than it may seem to give your power away. Parts of you and your energy can be pulled into external situations and other people's stories, dramas and needs without you realising it. When you allow other people's requests, decisions or beliefs to dictate how you feel about yourself, you have given away your power. If you say yes when you want to say no, you give your power away. All these moments and small decisions mount up and you can find yourself becoming very depleted. This in turn can cause you stress and even resentment as you don't have your full energy and resources at your disposal.

Pulling or drawing back into yourself enables you to claim back your power and stand in your strength. It feels very empowering to feel autonomous and from that space you can act and walk forward with your head held high.

I realised that I was giving my power away by doing too much for other people. Overcompensating, feeling responsible and, instead of supporting them, enabling them. I essentially taught them how to treat me by not speaking up, attempting to prevent issues and to fighting fires instead of putting them out by proclaiming destructive and unhealthy behaviours.

I wrote in my journal one day:

"I need to pull myself back in and realise that it's not healthy to give my power away. To give one man the power over my lovability and self-worth. I will no longer allow someone else's decisions to determine whether I am worthy of love or not. I claim myself. I claim my love."

To support you with recalling your energy back to you I have a free meditation available on my website: www.lindseyelms.com

The magic of words

How you speak to yourself and how other people speak to you has a profound effect. The adage *"sticks and stones may break my bones, but words will never hurt me"* is absolutely not true.

Words are like magic; they can create, and they can destroy.

Using positive words of love, compassion and affirmation creates an environment that encourages care. Negative words of blame, shame and criticism create an environment that encourages suffering and harm.

There are a couple of keywords in your vocabulary that can make a big difference to how you speak to yourself and view situations, they are 'why' and 'but'.

Why?

Asking yourself why is the quickest way I am aware of, to spiral yourself down into negative thinking and keep yourself stuck in the past. If you are confused by something or are wondering what has caused a feeling, often the word "why" will pop up.

Asking why directs your mind to look for answers, unfortunately as you are pre-programmed with a negative bias, the answers are most likely to be negative and self-deprecating.

For example:

Question

"Why did he leave?"

Answer

"Because I didn't try hard enough, wasn't sexy enough, didn't do/ earn/ show enough…Because he was…"

Asking why ties you up in knots because the answer is so subjective, especially if the person or situation is unable or unwilling to give you concrete answers.

A more useful word to use, a far less painful and much more positive one is how.

How?

Directing "how" questions inward with curiosity is a useful way to gain a positive perspective and help you to plan. "How" questions acknowledge an issue that needs addressing and invite you to be proactive.

Questions emerge such as:

- How can I think about what has happened constructively?
- How can I nurture myself through this hard time?
- How can I acknowledge what has happened without placing blame and move forward with grace?

But

"But" is an interesting little word that can have a negative effect. "But" in a sentence negates or cancels out what has been said in the previous part of the sentence. It can make a positive comment lose its warmth.

For example:

"I loved the restaurant you took me to, but the music was too loud."

The complimentary sentence started off so well and yet by using "but" in the middle and continuing with a negative conclusion, the whole sentence has lost its sparkle and original intent.

Yes, but...

Perhaps a friend has spent time sharing something heartfelt, intending to guide you. Then when they have finished sharing you say "Yes, but." That is the kind of response that makes the recipient's heart sink a little. It is like saying "I have been listening however I don't agree". It is not additive, it is subtractive.

But, but, but.

But can also play in your mind as a negative mantra and you can find yourself doing the "but" song that sounds like an engine attempting to start and backfiring, unable to move.

But I can't...

But what if...

But how will I...

The remedy to but is and.

And

The little word "and" can make a huge difference in a sentence, transforming it from subtractive to additive. From negative to positive. Using and in a sentence enables you to include more detail and information. To deepen awareness.

The mindful intention of using and instead of but can transform the way you speak to yourself and reply to other people.

Let's take the previous "but" sentence example and use and as a replacement:

"*I loved the restaurant you took me to, but the music was too loud.*"

"*I loved the restaurant you took me to and next time I would like to try out a quieter sort of ambience.*"

And for "Yes, but", an alternative could be:

"I have taken onboard what you have said, thank you and I agree with x, y. z points and I am still confused by...."

DR. EMOTO AND THE WONDERS OF WATER

I was first introduced to the effect of language on your mind and body when I came across the wonderful work of internationally acclaimed water researcher Dr. Masaru Emoto. Dr. Emoto conducted experiments with water crystals, the results of which are captivating and thought-provoking. He took samples of water and exposed them to words, pictures and music, both positive and negative. He then froze the water and looked at the crystal formations they made.

When he offered words like love, gratitude, beautiful, peace and joy, the resulting crystal patterns were beautiful and intricate. When Dr. Emoto offered negative words, such as hate, ugly, loathing, inadequate and abhorrent, the resulting crystals were unstructured and blob-like.

If you consider that your body is made up of at least 65% water and then think about the effects that words have on water, it can be a revelation. It's knowledge which may encourage you to use your words towards yourself and others with careful intention. To use more words of love as these experiments showed human thoughts and intentions can physically alter the molecular structure of water.

Your body is composed of upwards of 100 trillion cells and the more harmonious the vibrations in your body are, the healthier the body and mind is.

TAKE FIVE PAUSE AND ACTION

Write your favourite positive words of affirmation or terms of endearment such as love, beauty, and joy and place them around a bottle of water or underneath a glass of water and allow the vibration of the words to infuse the water. Then drink the water.

This is a lovely way of adding positive and loving vibrations to your body and mind. As well as acting as a reminder to speak kindly to yourself and others.

Chapter 13

THE DRAMA TRIANGLE

Taking a close look at your relationships to determine whether they are healthy or not is an important and courageous exercise. Even more so when you examine your role within them. It's common not to be consciously aware of how unhealthy, unproductive or toxic your relationships have become. Issues can creep up over time little by little without being detected or recognised.

Having an awareness of the drama triangle helps you to understand how you naturally respond to situations where you are attempting to get your needs met in unhealthy ways. Like me, you may not have been aware until now that your behaviours are inadvertently causing you additional suffering. By bidding for connection and support in specific unhealthy ways you are likely to be stepping into certain roles that continue the drama and pain.

This knowledge helps you to step out of the drama by recognising when you fall into a role and then choosing not to engage. This reduces the number of times you will find yourself feeling powerless and helpless. You will see the 'drama baton' being offered to you, be able to recognise it and choose not to pick it up.

The drama triangle is a model that describes how conflict arises between people, often in intense interactions where there is an unmet need. When in the drama, people will adopt one or more of the roles to try and control the situation and swing it in their favour. It was devised by Dr Stephen Karpman in 1968. The model has three roles that people participate in: the victim, rescuer, and persecutor.

THE VICTIM ROLE

This is the person who feels helpless or powerless, like they can never get ahead in life. They often think things like: *"This always happens to me"*, *"everyone's against me"*, *"it's not my fault"*, and: *"that's not fair."*

They can be defensive and unempathetic because their feelings are more important to them than other people's. They refuse to accept any responsibility for their situation often denying their role in it, no matter how small it may be. A simple "yes, hands up that was me" in these situations would go such a long way in defusing the tension.

They will give little or no effort, yet suggest that they have tried everything without success. They will often say: *"Yes, but..."* when others offer a solution to a problem, a response that is invalidating and dismissive.

They are the glass-half-empty people who believe that the world is against them, not for them. They will use countless excuses, dramatic language and body expressions to emphasise their made-up unfortunate circumstances. They find very little joy in life.

They can be ultra-sensitive to the most basic and harmless feedback and take it as a personal attack. They will defend themselves veraciously, sometimes going on the counterattack. Victims attempt to rally people around them to agree with their cause. They can be very ambiguous with their statements and go back and forth in making decisions which can be incredibly confusing.

Healing the Victim role

Consider and appreciate what you do have control over.

Think like a problem solver.

Look at yourself as a survivor, someone who is resilient.

The Rescuer role

This is the person who takes responsibility for other people's problems and makes them their own. Whilst at the same time they are not looking closely at their own lives which could be out of balance.

They say things like: *"I'm nice, I'll help them,"* or: *"If they just did what I say, they'd be happy."*

The rescuer wants to solve your problems and take on a caretaking role. However, if the help is not warranted or asked for, they may use guilt tactics to meet their needs. This can lead to resentment. The rescuer seeks out some sort of benefit from their efforts and if this is not forthcoming, you may hear them say things such as: *"After all I've done for you, this is how you treat me"*.

The rescuer has similarities to a peacekeeper, which is not part of the drama triangle although the concept can overlap. Whilst the peacekeeper is more inclined to do what it takes for the conflict to end, to have a positive resolution and harmony. The rescuer requires some sort of prize.

Healing the Rescuer role

Support instead of rescue — learn to become more of a teacher or a coach.

Stop the self-abandonment.

Learn to value yourself and take steps to increase your self-worth.

The Persecutor role

The persecutor is the person who is frustrated, they are self-righteous and tend to be a bit of a bully. Generally, the 'know it all' and the smartest cookie in the room. They are not shy about telling you how they think it is.

The persecutor criticises the enabling behaviours of the rescuer and blames the victim. They will shout from the mountain tops how much it is your fault and blame you for not following their way of doing things. They are the "I told you so" type, berating whilst shaking their heads in contempt.

They may think or say things like: *"They're wrong and I'm right"*, and: *"They need to do what I say."* They want to keep the victim down and focus on being right as they fear becoming a victim themselves. They can be controlling, disrespectful and nasty. They offer no real solutions to the problem as they stay up on their high horse.

Healing the Persecutor role

Challenge instead of criticising.

Encourage people instead of discouraging.

Have some patience and grace.

Take five Pause and Journal

After an encounter that has left you with unmet needs and feeling powerless, take some time to reflect on the experience. Take your mind back and observe yourself, like a fly on the wall.

Ask yourself the following questions and write down your thoughts as honestly as possible. Being honest with yourself will create greater awareness and more opportunities for healing.

- What was your role in the interaction?
- Did you change roles throughout the interaction between victim, rescuer and persecutor?
- What value did the role(s) bring to you?
- What actions can you now take? What limits or boundaries can you put in place?
- Do you find it difficult to say no? If so, practice saying no daily and write about how building up your 'no' muscle feels over 21 days.

Lindsey, the recovering Rescuer

I recognise myself most in the Rescuer role. My first response to my husband leaving was an attempt to rescue him from himself. To me he seemed sad and lost, and I felt a compulsion to help. I truly thought that if I didn't attempt to help I was abandoning him, and that would be going against my marriage vows.

I remember countless times when I would offer solutions to solve his reasons for leaving, attempting to show him a better way. I truly thought I could convince him that the "grass is greener where you water it" and that it was best for him to stay with me and our children.

What I didn't understand then was that I was allowing myself to be harmed in the name of love. In my misplaced understanding of love and commitment. I poured my love and energy into the potential. My whole perception of our marriage was built on hope, hope that 'love' would prevail. Hope that things would get better. Hope that he would show me the warmth he once did. Hope that I could get through with my words somehow. Now I know that this isn't love, the quality of true, tender love that is available to us all.

It wasn't until I stopped attempting to rescue him that two major learnings arose within me.

Firstly, people must find their own way in life. The optimal way for them to learn is through their own choices and decisions and grow based on their own life experiences. I wasn't helping by being the constant emotional blanket, cheerleader and problem solver.

Secondly, once I reclaimed my energy and stopped abandoning myself, I understood that I had been giving away far too much of my own energy. I had not been looking at how unhappy I had become, how helpless I felt, how much I craved emotional connection. By focusing outside of myself and how to hold onto my marriage, I had completely missed the fact I was participating in the role of rescuing to my detriment.

There were still the occasional times when I would get confused, fall back or get sucked into the Rescuer role, feeling guilty about saying no and putting myself first. I had to remind myself over and over again that self-preservation is a right. That just because someone engaged with me, I did not have to entertain them. I could stop tiptoeing around the feelings of someone who stamped all over mine and allow my heart to be heard.

The greatest gift you can give to yourself is self-love and self-compassion. When you love yourself exactly as you are, it is much more difficult for anyone to manipulate you or get under your skin.

For example, when I received texts months after we had separated that seemed sincere about wanting to talk, had an interest in me, or came with a hint of sadness, my resolve would weaken. I felt awkward and uneasy about upholding my boundaries and not re-engaging with someone who deeply hurt me and was no longer healthy for me. Once I understood the drama triangle, I was able to gain clarity and my resolve became a tower of strength.

Once I was able to see the games being played, I stepped out of the triangle. I felt no need to rescue, feel victimised or persecute. Instead, I chose to have compassion for myself, and all concerned and not give the situation any more of my precious energy.

When different layers of learning and healing appear now, perhaps triggered by a song, a random memory or a comment, I focus on acceptance and forgiveness. Acceptance and forgiveness are two choices that will need to be made, repeatedly until there are no more layers to heal. No more waves appearing in your usually calm emotional seas. I am mindful now to remember the lesson and not disappointments.

PART 4

Let your love shine

Chapter 14

LOVE

"Love is patient, love is kind. It does not envy, it does not boast, it is not proud. It does not dishonour others, it is not self-seeking, it is not easily angered, it keeps no record of wrongs. Love does not delight in evil but rejoices with the truth. It always protects, always trusts, always hopes, always perseveres."

- Corinthians, 13:5

Love is your core nature.

You are love incarnate.

I believe you come from love, you are love, you return to love and, in the middle, you can choose love.

Love is what sustains you, it is the soil you're planted in and the oxygen that fills your lungs.

Sometimes you can forget that you are loved and need to be reminded. Sometimes that reminder can be quite unexpected, a rude awakening that jolts you back into awareness. Other times it is gentle and nurturing like a warm summer breeze wafting across your face.

There's a saying: *"We see the world not as it is, but as we are"*. When you choose to see with love, you will see that the world is filled with love. Once you see that you are surrounded by love it becomes more and more uncomfortable to choose anything but love.

How do you let love in?

If somewhere along the line you had to protect yourself from hurt and pain, you may have closed your heart to truly feeling love again. You may now find it hard to let love in, even for yourself. When you are not able to feel love, it makes you feel separate and isolated. Love is a gift for everyone including you. It's your right to be connected to love and to bask in its warm embrace.

So, how do you let love in? The answer is to start with yourself. I believe that the best love stories are the ones not about our lovers but the tales of how we found ourselves. Ask yourself: Am I appreciating who I am? How much of what I express is so that someone else will like me? Who would I be if I didn't feel the need to hide, protect or defend?

It's not the situation you find yourself in that matters most, it's how you feel about yourself. You can absolutely still feel good about yourself whilst the world around you is throwing eggs. You can stand tall, be firm in your resolve and hold healthy boundaries. A tool I like to use is to imagine a sheet of clear plastic in front of myself, and every time an accusation, angry or hurtful words are thrown, see them as eggs splatting against the plastic and observe them running down, not touching or harming me.

How do I know how to let love in?

How can I stand steadfastly in this truth?

I know it from personal experience. I know that it is an absolute choice and the rewards for choosing love, to let love in are huge. I have learnt that to connect with people it's necessary to express my vulnerabilities.

I've discovered that when you intend to live in a loving way, to make decisions guided by love, it isn't always easy or immediately obvious how to go about it. It is a choice. It does not depend on your circumstances. It does not have to be an easy choice or the most obvious. You can make the choice no matter what is going on around you, for you. That's when the magic starts to happen.

I believed that choosing love meant upholding my marriage vows, and continuing to live by them even when my husband did not. I discovered that choosing to love meant giving myself permission to accept love, to invite it in for me. I chose to love me, for me. I decided to trust that I am lovable. I allowed what is to be enough. Not out of obligation, not out of greed or selfishness, simply out of love for me.

The rewards for making the choice surprised me. I was enlivened, filled up from the inside. This invigorated and brightened my life, appearing in many large and small ways. From the kindness of a lady at the supermarket who helped me out when I was 10 pence short for my shopping, to saying no to the old version of me. When I chose to let love in my whole world opened. A whole new world of possibilities, full of hope and faith in myself and my future life.

It was like shedding my old self to reveal the new me. In choosing love, I chose to let go of my old identity and create a new one. I no longer identified with the version of me that would tolerate being emotionally neglected, being told I wasn't good enough or doing enough and avoiding rocking the boat. I created a new map of my values and beliefs, guided by love and a strong resolve.

I was released from the confusion that I often felt which left me feeling small and unsure of myself. Confusion from words and behaviours that kept me down, stopping me from working out the truth of the situation, that I could choose an alternative: true love for myself, love born out of respect.

I was released from being grateful for the crumbs I received when I deserved the whole cake. I didn't even realise at the time I was settling for so much less than life and love wanted for me. I gained clarity in my mind and peace in my heart, which felt like a soft fluffy cloud where there was once a heavy storm cloud.

I gained a beautiful internal recognition, stemming from my heart and then radiating out like rays of the sun beaming outwards into my whole being and beyond. Recognition that felt like a warm cosy hug that said I can trust myself, that I can believe in myself and that I am fundamentally OK. An understanding that I have a lot to give and deserve all good things.

Love gives me a sense of pride that I am living life with integrity and grace.

Love gives me hope of continuously creating a meaningful and purposeful life where I achieve what I set out to do.

Love gives me faith that what's for me will not pass me by.

What gets in the way?

It can be disheartening when you have worked courageously through blood, sweat and tears to find that a negative situation, behaviour or pattern has further layers to learn from and heal.

Please know that you are not starting from scratch when a pattern or phase of a cycle reappears, you are deepening your awareness and healing. Take it as an opportunity for further growth and self-love.

Examples of what gets in the way of love and self-love are:

- ♥ You feel unworthy of true love
- ♥ You compare yourself to others
- ♥ You need validation from others
- ♥ Difficulty in making your own choices
- ♥ Difficulty expressing your needs

In these times remember:

Love is patient, love is kind.

Love encourages you to have patience and kindness for yourself and the situation. You are a work in progress as are we all. There may be moments where you may question yourself and that's OK. There may be moments where you feel anger or frustration bubble up from your newfound contentment and that's OK too. These moments are fleeting and if you allow yourself to let them flow, they will dissipate. Avoid grasping, pushing away or holding onto emotions; acknowledge them, name them. Once they have been given a voice and have been heard and understood, they will evolve.

It keeps no record of wrongs

Holding onto old stories and hurts and perhaps even using them against someone is harmful to you. It is not in alignment and integrity with who you are. Whilst you have likely lived through painful experiences, holding onto them to use as ammunition later takes up far too much precious space within you. Other people can sense resentment, anger and blame coming from you like a bad smell. You cannot hide it no matter how much you try to disguise it with nice scents in the form of flattery or disingenuous words.

Practising forgiveness is a wonderful antidote to any poison within you that is waiting to be dispensed. Forgiveness is for you. Forgiveness is a choice, not a feeling. It is facing the wrongs done to you, recognising the emotions inside and choosing not to hold it against the other person. Forgiveness allows you to take the poison out of the situation. It doesn't necessarily stop you from remembering. Instead, it enables you to make peace with it so that it is not front and centre in your mind anymore. No longer chewing you up, stirring your mind and emotions. It helps you to step out of the whirlwind around you and see it objectively for what it is.

From a place of calm and peace, the feeling of retribution is difficult to muster. Thus giving you more space, more bandwidth to concentrate on self-love and compassion. Forgiveness is a process that you will need to come back to often. It's a normal part of the healing process to keep forgiving the same hurt, sometimes daily.

Love does not delight in evil but rejoices with the truth

You know the truth of a situation, even if it starts with a subtle knowing from deep inside you and gains traction as you discover more information. You know the truth from your gut feeling, your intuition. If something feels off, then it's off!

When you have been bruised in life, emotions are likely to be a factor in your decision-making. In fact, most decisions are based on emotions from the car you drive, the house you live in and the amount of personal access you give to someone. Utilising truth enables you to make judgements and decisions without relying on emotion alone. To look at the facts first.

You can have compassion for a situation or person and still be unwavering in your resolve. It helps to have the facts in front of you that are as clear as day. If you find yourself wobbling when you have remained strong, I encourage you to revisit the facts of the situation and the actions a person took. Not the words that they said that may have been designed to get an emotional response, but the cold, hard facts.

It always protects, always trusts, always hopes, always perseveres.

Love protects you by making the act of being dishonoured uncomfortable. Love has no tricks and does not attempt to pull the wool over your eyes. Love is pure, true and honest. Love encourages you to trust yourself above all others. It gives you the flexibility to know when to trust someone and when to be discerning.

It always hopes for the best whilst being prepared for life to challenge your perceptions and expectations. It always perseveres by showing you that you are loved that you are Love and that you are worthy of its perseverance.

Loving and liking are not synonymous

Instead of focusing your energy on the loss of a relationship that wasn't as deep as you thought it was, where there were conflicting values, lack of compatibility, or involved abuse, you can choose to nurture and cultivate the most important relationships in your life now. And while keeping the door open for new ones.

You can have Love for someone, the same kind of Love you hold for all sentient beings and not like them anymore. You can choose who you are friends with. You can be friendly towards another person without being their friend. You can treat others with respect, even when they do not offer you the same.

TAKE FIVE PAUSE AND PRACTICE

Releasing the cords that bind

Guided meditation involving imagery is a very effective way of gently releasing energy that is not healthy for you to hold onto. The following meditation is a version of cord-cutting. It transforms the energy around a person or situation allowing more space for healing and growth.

Find a comfortable and upright posture.

Take some deep centring breaths.

Close your eyes and imagine sitting at the edge of a body of water at sunset. It could be the sea or a lake with a dock.

Feel the peace and calm wash over you as you take some deep releasing breaths.

Look out over the vast body of water and know that this chapter in your life is a mere drop or ripple and that there is so much more available to you.

As you scan your surroundings start to focus on something that has caught your eye and notice that it is a wooden boat tied up to a post.

As the boat bobs up and down on the gentle waves, consider what causes waves in your mind and emotions. What or who makes large waves that knock you off your course, off-centre?

Make the choice now to place into the boat anything or anyone that no longer serves your highest good. Decide that it is now time to release them with love.

Imagine filling up the boat until it is ready for its next journey, its next adventure with its passengers and cargo safe and happy inside.

You can see the passengers' faces and they are relaxed, there is no resistance or animosity around journeying onwards without you. They know it is best for all concerned.

Take hold of the rope that is securing the boat to the post and unwind the loops. As you unwind the rope, slowly releasing it from the post, acknowledge and give thanks for all the ways these threads of connection have benefited you.

Once the boat has been released from the post, place the rope inside the boat and allow it to float away.

Watch the boat as it floats further and further away from you. As it does so you notice that you feel lighter and lighter with a sense of freedom.

Watch the boat get closer and closer to the horizon as the sunset fades to dusk. The boat disappearing into the fading light.

Take some deep releasing breaths, knowing all is well. That part of your journey is now complete, and the passengers and cargo of the boat are free to also embark on their own separate journeys too.

Wiggle your fingers and wiggle your toes.

Gently blink open your eyes and come back into the room.

Notice what has changed, notice what is different.

Chapter 15

SOFTEN

> *"The trick to doing this is to stay with emotional distress without tightening into aversion, to let fear soften us rather than harden into resistance."*

> \- Pema Chodron

"Give them back", Molly shouted. The usual sibling argument was occurring upstairs or so it seemed.

"Give them back Oliver," she shrilled; this time her voice cracked a little which caught my attention. I was in the middle of a task that required my concentration and these outbursts were distracting me. Already feeling fragile, I was frustrated at having to put down what I was doing so that peace could reign again in the house.

As I reached the top of the stairs, I found both my children having a tug of war with a single white Nike sock. I could see and hear that Molly was getting more frustrated with her brother as he continued to hold onto the sock, somewhat bemused by her reaction and nonetheless determined to win.

"Just give her the sock back please," I said to Oliver as he let go. Molly, clearly distressed and overwhelmed from the exertion, shouted that "he shouldn't take her things," and ran away crying.

Still somewhat irritated by the whole drama, I had a chat with Oliver and then went to find Molly. I thought I'd find her in her bedroom, but she wasn't there. I checked my bedroom, the living room, the den and garden, but she was nowhere to be seen. At that point I got a bit concerned; she was clearly upset by more than the loss of a single sock.

I called out her name — silence.

Then out of the corner of my eye, I saw something move in my walk-in wardrobe. The doors were slightly ajar and there she was; my beautiful girl, curled up in the corner, sobbing her heart out. Sat in a ball with her knees bent up, her arms folded together and her head resting on top of them. My heart sank to my toes as I could sense the pain she was in.

All of the frustration and tension I had, and the thoughts about the kids wasting my time melted away instantly, replaced with love, concern and compassion. I softened.

I opened the door and she looked up at me, tears rolling down her anguished face. She unfolded her arms and held them out to me as I knelt in front of her and took her in my arms. I held her close and sat with her until she felt better. I understood that her deeper suffering was the loss of her dad, that she felt that life as she knew it had been taken away from her. She was holding onto the sock because she didn't want the pain and distress of anything else being taken from her.

This experience; taking the time to slow down, to feel into and connect with what was going on and with my children was poignant. It deepened our relationship at a really stressful and hard time for all of us. I chose to soften instead of hardening. To seek to open my heart instead of close it. To stay with the pain and to understand it until it was no longer something to be feared. To hold space for emotions to flow for the benefit of myself and my children.

Choice point

When you have been hurt, betrayed or let down you have a choice; let hurt harden you or let hurt soften you. There's a saying: *"boiling water can soften potatoes and harden an egg."* It's a testament to your character as to how you chose to respond when life heats up to boiling point.

You have the choice to allow the hurt and pressure to be utilised in a positive way. To soften in your response, in heart and mind.

TAKE FIVE PAUSE AND PRACTICE

Soften exercise

Remember that reading something offers one level of awareness, whilst practising or doing something really helps you to embed the learning. I invite you to take a pause, to put away or minimise any distractions and to be present in the moment.

Place your feet on the ground and sit in a comfortable, upright and alert position. Relax your shoulders and jaw and take a few deep belly breaths. Then have a go at the practice offered below.

Soften mantra

When you notice that you are being hard on yourself or a situation, a useful mantra to refocus your thoughts is "*soften*". The word itself repeated slowly several times can encourage a softening of tension in your body and to bring awareness of any negativity or criticism that is swirling around your mind.

Repeat the word "**Soften**" slowly and softly.

Soften

Notice the images that pop up in your mind.

Soften

Notice the warmth that radiates out from your heart.

Soften

Notice how your body takes a big deep breath.

Soften

Notice how your shoulders release and your jaw relaxes.

Soften

Notice the peaceful sensation that washes over your body and mind.

When an experience is difficult, you can fight with it. In the moment, your natural instincts are likely to tell you to be hard, to put up your walls and close your heart. What if, instead, you surrender to it? Let down your walls and be open to the experience? You will grow from the pain by giving up the hard walls you have surrounded yourself with and softening your heart and mind to what comes your way.

Learning to relax with life, to go with the flow rather than against the current and to see what happens from a place of softness, enables you to make decisions with more wisdom. To take actions with more power than if you were fighting. Remember when you are in a calm, balanced state you have access to all your resources, as opposed to when your system is stressed and shut down.

Consider what would softening look like in this moment?

What could result from softening?

Who might you become?

Soften practice

Make a tight fist. Now soften your hand and let it open and expand.

Repeat making a fist and this time notice the sensation of release, relaxation and unfurling. Notice the lightness, the sensation of unfolding and expansion. Imagine it like a flower bud opening.

Now do the same with your neck and shoulders, just for a moment. Raise your shoulders towards your ears and tighten them. Feel how compressed your whole body becomes. And release the tightness, slowly and gently. Notice how much more space and openness has been created.

Without adding more tension this time, simply ask for another level of relaxation and unwinding in your shoulders. Notice how you feel emotionally when you do this.

Soften acronym

Acronyms are a great way to remember the essence of an idea. I hope you find this one useful to remember the importance of softening.

Suffering

Open up

Face it

Tell yourself a different story

Empathy

Notice

Slow down and notice your suffering

Something that causes you to experience fear or hurt creates suffering. It could be a comment someone has made, a negative experience, or a fear about the future. Your likely first reaction is to want to shut down, to tighten up, to make it go away. The invitation here is to slow down and to notice that you are suffering. To take a moment to feel that fear. To notice that you want to harden in order to protect yourself.

How do you know that you are suffering if you don't give yourself the opportunity to slow down long enough to recognise it?

John Lennon is quoted as saying: *"Life is what happens whilst you're busy doing other things."*

Life is a gift, and by attempting to bypass suffering, you are inadvertently missing out on the treasures it is offering you. Sitting with your pain and suffering long enough to listen to and understand what it is telling you, is valuable.

By slowing down, you allow yourself to simply be — you are, after all a human being not a human doing.

Open up

Instead of hardening, choose to open up to the emotions that are causing you fear and discomfort. Open to kindness, compassion and love. Opening to something involves letting it in. To expand rather than contract. Like unlocking a door and opening it to reveal what is on the other side. Opening involves a level of courage and vulnerability. To explore the unknown. Notice how your body feels. Is it tense and contracted or is it open and relaxed? Notice what thoughts are playing in your mind. Are they positive and light or are they negative and heavy?

Consider what opens you up; what kinds of thoughts, feelings, experiences and sensations enable you to expand? Could it be the sound of a child laughing? Watching spring lambs playing? An elderly couple walking down the street arm in arm?

When you open your heart, you will sense it as a warm glow in your chest, like a big sunshine radiating out of your heart space.

Face it

Once you allow yourself to notice the scary thoughts, you can face them and explore them. You can begin to unpick the fear and see it for what it is. To perceive it from a different angle. Where before it seemed large and looming, in the light of awareness, what you were afraid of is likely to be smaller than you imagined.

There are several acronyms for the word fear:

- False Evidence Appearing Real,
- Forget Everything And Run,
- Face Everything And Rise.

Whilst forgetting everything and running may seem at first like an appealing option, it doesn't solve anything. Facing your fear, looking it square in the eyes and not removing your gaze until it isn't daunting anymore enables you to rise above it.

Use the concept of false evidence appearing real to help you. Ask yourself some questions to uncover any potential masks this fear has been hiding behind. Can you disprove or add doubt to the thoughts that wanted to remain rigid?

Beliefs are only thoughts that you have said or heard many times over and have been made true. The word "belief" has "lie" in the middle; where then can you find the lie? Asking yourself questions like "Is it really true?" "What proof do I have?" and "Where's the evidence?" enables you to see beliefs, thoughts and situations from different perspectives and therefore relaxes their grip on you.

Tell yourself a different story

You can gain insights into your own suffering by noticing the thoughts you are thinking and the stories you are telling yourself. Are you spending time worrying and making up stories in your mind about what may happen? Or reliving something unpleasant from the past? In an anxious state you may get stuck in the details, and get carried away with the negative feelings and so to attempt to feel better you drift away into a fantasy, story or planning. That approach seems to offer comfort and the promise of feeling more secure. Yet it can often serve to dig you deeper into suffering.

The good news is that you can put those stories down, choose to leave them alone, allow them to fade away, and then tell yourself a different story. Focus on one that is more empowering, kind and compassionate.

Where can you change the narrative?

When telling yourself reasons to be angry, hurt or closed down, what can you now say to bring in compassion?

Rather than telling yourself that you were wrong, foolish, duped. Tell the story of wanting to see the best in someone. That you trusted until you were given reason to create healthier boundaries.

Instead of judgment, blame or shame, where can you replace your thoughts, words and stories with kindness, forgiveness and understanding?

Empathy

Empathy is walking in someone else's shoes to find out how a situation felt or was experienced. To understand it from their point of view rather than your own. This skill generates curiosity, to listen with the intention of understanding and with an open mind. Acknowledge and validate the feelings involved by saying phrases like: "I'm sorry you are going through this". Use empathy as an opportunity to learn something about yourself, the other person or the situation that you were not aware of before.

Be sure that you are using empathy and not sympathy. A psychology tutor once told me a story about the difference between the two which has really stuck with me.

> A man was walking along and came across a deep hole, he heard a boy shouting for help. As he peered over the side, he could see the boy encased, trapped at the bottom with no way out. The man jumps into the hole and reassures him. He feels sorry for the boy and yet he is no real help to him because now he is in the same predicament. This is sympathy.

> A lady comes along the path and hears the cries for help from the man and the boy. She peers into the hole and sees them both at the bottom. She wants to help and understands that they are scared. She looks around and finds some rope, ties it to a tree and throws down the rope to the man and boy. They use the rope to pull themselves out and at the top she listens to their ordeal and offers them a cuppa. This is empathy.

Notice

Now that you have taken a moment to slow down and acknowledge something scary that is causing suffering; opened to the sensations and faced the fear eye to eye, then told yourself a different story whilst bringing in empathy; you can put it all together and notice the change. What is different now?

Energy follows focus. Or another way to say this is: your energy flows where your attention goes. For example, if you put your attention on your feet that's where your energy goes, and you notice all the sensations in your feet such as warmth and tingling. Have a go and notice.

What has changed?

What feelings, thoughts, and sensations are different now through practising the process of soften?

How have these new insights given you nourishment? Food for thought to help you grow and prosper?

Write down in your journal or notepad any insights or 'Aha' moments that you would benefit from remembering.

Chapter 16

9 STAR KI YEARS — EVERYTHING IN GOOD TIME

Nine stages of transformation

When you have been through a big change and life seems uncertain, knowing that the phase you are in will not last indefinitely can be comforting. Knowing that there is a plan, a structure that you can use as a guiding light or North Star, offers a sense of assurance.

Each year of the nine-year cycle brings a different focus. A different theme. A chance to learn and grow in nine different areas from potential to full steam ahead. Being aware of and intentionally working with the theme of the year enables you to use time to your advantage; to ride the wave.

The theme of each year supports planning ahead and offers insight into the types of experiences you are likely to have, including emotionally. Having an awareness of what you are stepping into can be very helpful. If you know what you'll likely encounter, what to expect and the energy behind it, it makes life so much easier. You can rest into it, like allowing yourself to be supported in the arms of a comfy sofa and wrapped up in a warm cosy blanket. Occasionally you may need to adjust, get some water and have a stretch and yet overall, you feel assured.

Each year has a metaphorical season associated with it, which carries certain qualities and imagery. It is a cycle so you can use it to understand where you have been, where you are now and where you are going.

I have provided the dates for your next two nine-year cyclic themes in the following pages. To discover subsequent years simply add nine. For example, if your birth number is 1 Water and you're in the year 2023, the theme of the year is strategy. This theme will then reoccur in 2032, 2041, 2050, 2059 and so on.

ONE YEAR: POTENTIAL/ DREAMING

Observe and dream

If your birth number is 1: 2022, 2031, 2040

If your birth number is 2: 2021, 2030, 2039

If your birth number is 3: 2020, 2029, 2038

If your birth number is 4: 2019, 2028, 2037

If your birth number is 5: 2018, 2027, 2036

If your birth number is 6: 2017. 2026, 2035

If your birth number is 7: 2016, 2025, 2034

If your birth number is 8: 2015, 2024, 2033

If your birth number is 9: 2014, 2023, 2032

The One Year invites you to slow down, go within and spend time in reflection, prayer and meditation. This year is associated with the energy of winter where it seems like nothing is growing when actually the seeds are soaking up rich nutrients in preparation for spring. It can be a very nourishing time to gestate, receive and deepen your connection with yourself and the source of Life. This is a great year to learn, develop a skill and study, to allow yourself time to imagine and dream about what you can create in future months and years.

Things will not happen quickly this year, so be prepared for some frustration and opportunities for patience. Your intuition will be greatly heightened this year. You may encounter lessons that enable you to take back your personal power and discover who you are. Your intuition will help you make decisions from love not fear.

This year is a chance to explore lifelong beliefs around your value and worth and to find a deeper more meaningful love for yourself. You may have experiences that dissolve old ways of doing things that no longer serve you so that you can become the best version of yourself. To encourage your authentic self to surface more and more.

TWO YEAR: STRATEGY

Plan and nurture

If your birth number is 1: 2023, 2032, 2041

If your birth number is 2: 2022, 2031, 2040

If your birth number is 3: 2021, 2030, 2039

If your birth number is 4: 2020, 2029, 2038

If your birth number is 5: 2019, 2028, 2037

If your birth number is 6: 2018, 2027, 2036

If your birth number is 7: 2017, 2026, 2035

If your birth number is 8: 2016, 2025, 2034

If your birth number is 9: 2015, 2024, 2033

After the reflection and dreaming of the One Year, the Two Year is all about building the foundations for the future. You may feel like things have stagnated, however this pause is a chance to connect, practice patience and plan. This year is associated with the energy of late summer. It's that quiet period between noon and 3 pm — a favourite time for a little nap.

A Two Year is a good time to get your ducks in a row and create a strategy. Decide on the ideal ways you want to show up and serve. Once you have decided on a way ahead, look out for mentors or people offering support and help. This is a year where helpers are likely to show up in serendipitous ways.

Whilst you are in this period of downtime, it's a great opportunity to consider any obstructions in your life. What interferes with everything going smoothly? Ensure that you give from your overflow and maintain healthy boundaries during this year. It's a really good time to consider what makes you feel truly loved and nurtured. If you are not balanced around nurturing ask yourself, how can I receive more? Turn love inward and enjoy the things in life that bring you comfort and pleasure. Have a massage or a spa day, go on your favourite hike, eat delicious food and bring the family together.

Get everything prepared and think through your plans as next year it's time for lift-off!

THREE YEAR: LET'S GO

Rise and proceed

If your birth number is 1: 2015, 2024, 2033

If your birth number is 2: 2014, 2023, 2032

If your birth number is 3: 2022, 2031, 2040

If your birth number is 4: 2021, 2030, 2039

If your birth number is 5: 2020,2029, 2038

If your birth number is 6: 2019, 2028, 2037

If your birth number is 7: 2018, 2027, 2036

If your birth number is 8: 2017, 2026, 2035

If your birth number is 9: 2016, 2025, 2034

This is a year of new possibilities fuelled by the energy of sunrise and springtime, symbolic of new growth and development. After the planning stages of the last two years (1 Water and 2 Earth), you can now start to put those plans into action. Ideas are springing up like the emergence of new shoots in spring. It's a year of vibrant, rising energy. Lots of ideas will be popping up in your mind and not all of them will go the distance. Like a plethora of baby sea turtles clambering from the beach to the sea, many will make it however not all.

The slower pace of the last two years is replaced by enthusiasm, and you will feel impulsive and confident. Be fearless and try new things. With such rapid progress, being successful in your endeavours will require you to keep an eye on the details and remain focused on your goals.

This is a perfect year to initiate a new project or go on an adventure. Give things a go and get feedback from them. If it doesn't work, move forward onto the next idea. Don't get stuck in stagnation or overthinking. Your enthusiasm will be an inspiration to others. Remember with all this activity to slow down now and then, give yourself time to relax, perhaps on a Sunday afternoon.

FOUR YEAR: GROWTH

Rapid growth and development

If your birth number is 1: 2016, 2025, 2034

If your birth number is 2: 2015, 2024, 2033

If your birth number is 3: 2023, 2032, 2041

If your birth number is 4: 2022, 2031, 2040

If your birth number is 5: 2021, 2030, 2039

If your birth number is 6: 2020, 2029, 2038

If your birth number is 7: 2019, 2028, 2037

If your birth number is 8: 2018, 2027, 2036

If your birth number is 9: 2017, 2026, 2035

This is the second year in a two-year cycle of growth and change that started in your Three Year. Now that your ideas have pushed through and made the distance, it's time to cultivate them into projects. It's time to flesh out your ideas and take the next steps. Ideally its best to stay focused on the general direction you started last year, to build on it. Persevere and do not throw in the towel if you hit any roadblocks.

Staying focused may prove to be tricky at times as this year the direction that you thought you were heading in can suddenly change. It can feel like an uncertain time where you are indecisive and unsure, like everything is up in the air. You may even have the rug pulled out from under you in some way. An image for the 4 Tree is wind, and this energy can feel like it's blowing you around and even off course.

Know though that wonderful things are happening this year, sometimes the wind needs to shake things up a little to get you on the right path. Avoid impulsive actions or procrastination and develop a practice of compassion and patience with yourself. Stay grounded and get some advice where needed. This year you can be influential as well as influenced, elders or wise people are likely to show up and help.

FIVE YEAR: IN THE CENTRE

Pause and balance

If your birth number is 1: 2017, 2026, 2035

If your birth number is 2: 2016, 2025, 2034

If your birth number is 3: 2015, 2024, 2033

If your birth number is 4: 2023, 2032, 2041

If your birth number is 5: 2022, 2031, 2040

If your birth number is 6: 2021, 2030, 2039

If your birth number is 7: 2020, 2029, 2038

If your birth number is 8: 2019, 2028, 2037

If your birth number is 9: 2018, 2027, 2036

In a 5 Earth year it can feel like everything is coming towards you all at once. Experiences, offers, and new opportunities present themselves seemingly out of nowhere. This can cause you to be unsure about which way to go. It's advisable not to take any wild or frantic actions or be overindulgent. It can be an unpredictable and emotional year that can feel like a rollercoaster with big ups and downs.

The key to navigating this year is to remain still and centred and allow things to come to you as much as possible. Aim to avoid long journeys or moving home. The energy of this year is focused on centring yourself and it can be distracting to make large movements.

It is a year to pause, a time to reassess and analyse. Evaluate the systems you are using in your life from how you do your food shopping to your exercise routine. Are there any tweaks that you can make so that you can fully express yourself? A Five Year is a great time to find yourself and understand your potential. It is a powerful year for growth and healing. A time when you can see connections and how things tie in together, like cause and effect.

New projects that are initiated this year are likely to do very well and have a lasting effect. Along with this, you may also find that offers of help and support from unexpected sources arrive and pleasantly surprise you. A great combination for success.

SIX YEAR: CLARITY AND FOCUS

Own your power

If your birth number is 1: 2018, 2027, 2036

If your birth number is 2: 2017, 2026, 2035

If your birth number is 3: 2016, 2025, 2034

If your birth number is 4: 2015, 2024, 2033

If your birth number is 5: 2023, 2032, 2041

If your birth number is 6: 2022, 2031, 2040

If your birth number is 7: 2021, 2030, 2039

If your birth number is 8: 2020, 2029, 2038

If your birth number is 9: 2019, 2028, 2037

In your Six Year it is typical that you will achieve a new level in your life, perhaps in your career by getting a promotion or retiring or completing a project that is close to your heart. With a growing sense of pride from standing in your power, your skills and talents will be noticed by others. Rewards come to you from the outside world, you'll feel like you have stepped up.

Lead by example, be structured and organised. Let your work express the best of what you can give. This year you have the capacity to focus and get things done, and you will be confident about your endeavours. Reflect on your vision of the future, of your ideal life. Refine your definition of what your ideal life is all about. Ask yourself: "Who did I come here to be and what do I want?" This focus enables you to make clear decisions.

Having an authentic purpose helps to raise self-worth and self-esteem. Don't let the anxiety of looking after everyone else stop you from taking care of yourself. Make a conscious effort to tune in and understand the intentions of others whilst focusing on your goals. Communicate in a way that is not overbearing or overly opinionated.

Take time to meditate and breathe. To be able to sit in stillness and quiet takes strength. It's active, not passive. It's a strong, active state. Space clearing or energy clearing are great ways to clear out any stagnant energy to help you connect and gain clarity. Tidying up your space and having a sort-out, are simple ways of doing this.

SEVEN YEAR: REAPING REWARDS

Joy and harvest

If your birth number is 1: 2019, 2028, 2037

If your birth number is 2: 2018, 2027, 2036

If your birth number is 3: 2017, 2026, 2035

If your birth number is 4: 2016, 2025, 2034

If your birth number is 5: 2015, 2024, 2033

If your birth number is 6: 2014, 2023, 2032

If your birth number is 7: 2022, 2031, 2040

If your birth number is 8: 2021, 2030, 2039

If your birth number is 9: 2020, 2029, 2038

All your efforts over the last few years are now coming together and bearing fruit. It is time for you to receive and celebrate so allow yourself to be open to receiving. It may seem like things are coming to you quite effortlessly however this is a direct result of previous effort so find ways to enjoy it.

Take time for celebration, pleasure and self-reward, buy yourself a lovely gift, cook, or go out and enjoy beautiful food. Be careful of being too frivolous or taking your good fortune for granted, enjoy it but maintain a good balance. You can treat yourself without upsetting your bank balance.

This can be a very inspirational time for you, a chance to experience beauty such as going out in nature, visiting art galleries or having a good massage. Soak up the preciousness of life by watching butterflies dancing around a Buddleia in full bloom, wear your favourite clothes, use your best tableware and spend time with those you love.

This year reflect on what brings you joy. What brings you pleasure, inspiration and appreciation. Emotionally guard against feelings of sadness due to nostalgia or worry over deprivation, remember our minds can flip to the negative when we appear to be having too much fun! It is right and good to reap what you deserve, perhaps just avoid making careless choices and decisions whilst embracing joy and pleasure.

EIGHT YEAR: DEEP CHANGE AND TRANSFORMATION

Time to gather

If your birth number is 1: 2020, 2029, 2038

If your birth number is 2: 2019, 2028, 2037

If your birth number is 3: 2018, 2027, 2036

If your birth number is 4: 2017, 2026, 2035

If your birth number is 5: 2016, 2025, 2034

If your birth number is 6: 2015, 2024, 2033

If your birth number is 7: 2023, 2032, 2041

If your birth number is 8: 2022, 2031, 2040

If your birth number is 9: 2021, 2030, 2039

The seeds of change are stirring and, just like a caterpillar transforming into a butterfly, this year may not be comfortable, yet the result is likely to be beautiful. At first it may seem like things just aren't right and this will develop into a deep re-evaluation. This year you will be confronted by all the ways you are not feeling fulfilled. It's OK, you don't have to rush and change everything right now, Eight Year energy shines a light on the veiled areas, so be aware and notice. Then you can begin to change in small, measured ways. The change is designed to give you an opportunity to be aligned and happy.

An Eight Year is a year of evaluation, to consider what is not working and gather information. Allow quiet time for walks, pondering, study and research. Have plenty of cave time otherwise you are likely to get angry and stomp your feet. Making small changes can help with the frustration, like having your hair cut, getting a tattoo or rearranging the furniture.

Trust the process; it can be a struggle and you may feel resistance as it's difficult to wait and see what's waiting to be born. Attempt to let go. Frustration is a strong motivator, and you may go into task mode; serious and responsible. There can be some communication issues so double check emails, dates and plans. Be mindful to soften any stubbornness, mountains can be moved with love.

NINE YEAR: FIRE

In the spotlight

If your birth number is 1: 2021, 2030, 2039

If your birth number is 2: 2020, 2029, 2038

If your birth number is 3: 2019, 2028, 2037

If your birth number is 4: 2018, 2027, 2036

If your birth number is 5: 2017, 2026, 2035

If your birth number is 6: 2016, 2025, 2034

If your birth number is 7: 2015, 2024, 2033

If your birth number is 8 2023, 2032, 2041

If your birth number is 9: 2022, 2031, 2040

Here comes the Sun! After the reorientation of the previous year, you are entering a year of full expansion and rapid movement. You'll spend your time either full speed ahead or crashed out from exertion. You have a newfound clarity; the clouds have lifted and new ideas and opportunities surface and come to light.

You have now come full circle and all paths become visible. It is a time of completion; some things may come to an end such as projects, jobs or friendships. It is time to put everything into the fire of transformation ready for the next nine-year cycle to begin.

This year is filled with the energy of optimism, clarity, enthusiasm and adventure. A great time for fame and recognition, to get easily noticed. Make use of this time being in the spotlight — it is a good year to powerfully publicise yourself. Have fun, be social and do things that bring you joy.

As the bright light of clarity illuminates everything around you, there is the possibility of some secrets or frailties that you would prefer to remain hidden being brought to light. It is also possible to get overwhelmed by everything that is going on in your hectic year, so slow down now and then to bring projects to a conclusion before following the next shiny object.

Chapter 17

NINE KEY SELF-SOOTHING TOOLS

Self-soothing encapsulates all the ways that you can comfort yourself when thoughts and emotions are overwhelming. Self-soothing is a healing balm that you can give to yourself. Like a warm hug or blanket that wraps around you, holds you close and lets you know that everything is going to be OK. Self-soothing helps you regulate your emotional state and learning how to do it can be an invaluable skill during times of stress and uncertainty.

If you're having a tough time right now, it can feel like there is nothing you can do. I promise you there is. There are so many things you can do to help yourself feel better. Self-soothing is available to you night or day, all you need to do is choose which activity meets your needs in the moment. You may find that you develop a favourite or two and they become your go-tos. Some may seem quite simple, and they are. Sometimes the simplest of things have the most profound results.

When I was at my lowest points, scared, confused and heartbroken using these tools helped me through. They enabled me to fall asleep when I lay in bed in the dark feeling alone and ashamed, and they gave me strength to face another day by building my confidence and clarity.

Self-soothing activities help you feel safe in your body, regulate your emotions, and cope with distressing thoughts and feelings. They activate your parasympathetic nervous system, the soothing state that your body and mind have to rest and digest.

There are many ways to self-soothe including breathing techniques, listening to music, sipping a cup of herbal tea like camomile (I like mine with some honey), petting your dog or cat and walking out in nature. The following nine tools can be used interchangeably with the activities just mentioned.

I'd encourage you to have a go at as many as possible and then regularly practice your favourites.

1. JOURNALLING

Journalling or writing your thoughts onto a page is one of the best tools I know to work through and alleviate suffering.

Seeing your thoughts as words reflected back to you is incredibly empowering and insightful. Rather than having the ruminating thoughts swirl around your mind causing havoc, you can observe and catch them. It's like reaching up and catching them in your hand like you would a dandelion seed to make a wish. Any thoughts that no longer serve you can be gently blown away by the breeze as the wind catches them.

Journalling offers you the opportunity to hold your words on the page as they whisper their magical truth to you. Their sparkly glints of wisdom winking at you.

Simply being and sitting with your own thoughts is a gift to yourself which allows you the time and space to reflect without the noise and distraction of other energies around you. It has enabled me to hear my own voice, the one that was barely audible before.

Journalling involves slowing down and an inner honesty. You know your truth, yet sometimes it takes a bit of intention and courage to uncover it. Yes, it's scary and uncomfortable at times — I can hear your reservations. If you sit with the feelings and let them flow through your words, they will dissipate, and you will create more space and peace within you.

Writing down your innermost thoughts does not need to be neat and tidy. There's no requirement for correct spelling and good grammar. Your words can be angry, sad or happy. You can scribble them down hard and fast like there's steam coming off your pen or you can take your time like a meandering walk along a river. The amount of time you spend on it is also up to you — five minutes or three hours, you're in charge. The key thing is to give it a go and let the wonders of journalling unfold.

If sitting with a blank page feels daunting start with a prompt. Here are a few to get you started.

- ♥ The best things happening in my life now are…
- ♥ I am frustrated, resistant, annoyed about…
- ♥ I feel confused about…
- ♥ I want…

2. SELF-LOVE

Connect to the magic of you

You may associate self-love with hot bubble baths, having a massage or drinking a luxurious hot chocolate with marshmallows. Whilst these are all wonderfully soothing and highly recommended, they don't involve connecting with your true self; the magic of you.

Experiences like divorce, redundancy, or the kids moving out of home can cause you to search for your centre again. Without the focus you were so accustomed to, you may feel a sense of emptiness that you don't quite know how to fill. This can be experienced in a variety of ways including a lack of identity and a feeling of instability. Cultivating a strong sense of self, gives you the centre you have been missing.

Self-love means accepting yourself as you are, for everything that you are. Self-love is a state of appreciation for yourself that grows from actions that support your physical, emotional and spiritual growth. It means putting yourself first and having a high regard for your own well-being and happiness.

Self-love means taking care of your own needs and not sacrificing who you are or your well-being to please others.

Self-love means not settling for less than you deserve.

How do you know if you need more self-love?

- ♥ You feel unworthy of love.
- ♥ You feel that you are not good enough for your ideal partner.
- ♥ You compare yourself to others.
- ♥ Difficulty in speaking up for your own needs.
- ♥ Needing validation from others.
- ♥ Striving to impress so that you'll be liked.

If any of those statements ring true for you, the good news is that adding more self-love is the antidote. When you truly love yourself for who you are, there's no desire to compare or strive to impress — you will stand tall in your truth. With your self-love levels topped up, you are able to express your needs and know you are worthy of true love.

Self-Love Reminder Tool

A simple and effective way of building your self-love muscles is to remind yourself weekly or daily what you love about yourself.

Write down five things that you love about yourself, using your name.

For example:

I love you Lindsey because you are thoughtful.

- ♥ _____
- ♥ _____
- ♥ _____
- ♥ _____
- ♥ _____

Now read out loud what you have written and notice a gentle smile appear on your face and a warm glow radiate from your heart.

3. EMBRACE VULNERABILITY

Ask yourself: "What about me?"

Vulnerability is the willingness to be open, to show your emotions and share your insecurities. Being vulnerable can be very challenging. It can feel unsafe, exposing, and even shameful when something has changed in your life that you weren't prepared for. Vulnerability has been portrayed as a negative thing by past generations and in the UK, the idea of the stiff upper lip has immortalised it. Therefore, you might have grown up with the message that being vulnerable is wrong or not appropriate.

Whilst you may face barriers to embracing vulnerability such as a past experience of rejection or having an emotionally unavailable parent, cultivating this skill and becoming more emotionally available will enhance and deepen your relationships. It opens the doors to you connecting deeply with yourself and people who nurture your well-being.

Being vulnerable allows you to access your suffering and express it. To bring to light what is causing you pain, uncertainty or fear, provides you with the opportunity to be held and supported through it.

It's a beautiful gift to share your genuine thoughts and feelings. If you cope with life's challenges by bottling it all up, you may be festering resentment, or avoiding being honest about how you feel to yourself and others.

Vulnerability can provide a sense of belonging which is essential to your well-being. If you seek to discover your barriers to openness, you can take steps to overcome them and enjoy a better sense of connection. Speaking from your heart and sharing details about you and your life allows the listener to understand you at a deeper level.

When your vulnerability is met with compassion and caring, the reward is priceless. It bestows a wonderful feeling of being validated and understood. Embracing vulnerability helps the people around you do the same and can cultivate intimacy and trust in your relationships.

Embracing vulnerability did not come easy to me. I resisted it because it felt too scary, and partly because it wasn't welcomed or supported in my marriage. If you were taught as a child to be 'nice', to be 'good' and 'not to rock the boat'; in adulthood that message can be translated to" people will only like or love me if I am 'good.' That is what I believed.

The question "What about me?" popped into my mind quite often in the months leading up to the separation. I noticed that I was consistently being put on the bottom of the priority list, left on the sidelines unless it had been deemed I had done or achieved something 'good'.

I could feel the contrast between interest and disappointment radiating out from him. On the days when I mentioned I had created income for the household, there was interest and praise. On the days I had excitedly listed what I had done for me or to build my business, there was an air of displeasure. I remember the squirmy sensation at the pit of my stomach when he asked what jobs had been done around the house or what was for dinner rather than celebrating my achievements with me.

At first, I considered the thought "What about me?" a little childish, as though I was whining or being selfish. Then I realised that it was much bigger and deeper than that. Once I truly understood the gravity of what I was asking of myself and how honestly answering this question would affect my life — i.e. a radical change — the question gained momentum in my system. My self-worth had been activated, going from being quite dormant to being awakened. When I began to lightly question him about my concerns and what we could do about them, it wasn't too long before he chose to discard me.

"What about me?" Is a question that is generally posed when you are feeling very depleted; when you've reached the last straw. It can be triggered by something so small, yet underneath this question is a sea of unmet needs. Your needs can only truly be met by you. However, it's important to be brave and communicate them to others as well.

It's better to know the truth than to live a lie. To know who welcomes your authenticity and honesty and who does not value it. Vulnerability received and held in a loving, caring way is a beautiful gift to give someone. Vulnerability in the hands of someone who has earned your trust, who sees your inner and outer beauty, melts away any misgivings. Vulnerability is worth the effort. I'm so glad I can now use it as one of my superpowers. I hope you choose to give yourself the same self-love.

4. CREATE SPACE

A calming space can help reduce stress levels and promote relaxation and peace. When you have a busy mind, are feeling angry, confused or distressed, creating space helps to disentangle from the noise and re-centre.

Taking a break can de-escalate your emotions or anxiety before you reach overwhelm. If you have reached boiling point or have been triggered, taking yourself somewhere quiet can be very soothing.

There are often days or weeks when it seems like everything is going wrong or everyone wants something from us; this is particularly hard if you are a newly single mum for example. Your head can feel like it is literally filling up with so many thoughts and to do's that you may drown in them. By creating some space, you can decompress, which allows solutions to pop more easily into your mind.

There are many ways you can create space, here are a few suggestions:

- ♥ Create a clean, tidy and quiet area in your home where you won't be disturbed. One that is comfortable and cosy enough for you to let go and relax.
- ♥ Go to a local spa and have a massage or sauna.
- ♥ Meditate, listen to music or a podcast.
- ♥ Walk in nature.

Space can also feel uncomfortable before you've experienced the benefits. At first, having some time alone can seem like a waste of time because you could be doing so many other things. At times the quiet can be deafening because you are confronted with loneliness and a sense of emptiness that was once so easily filled or disregarded. It can feel unnerving because it encourages you to be with yourself.

Being with yourself is wonderful if you allow it to be.

Consider this:

You will always have yourself.

This means that you are always there for you, no matter what. Making friends with yourself, being kind to yourself and learning to enjoy your own company are forms of self-love.

Create space for self-discovery

Creating space enables you to self-inquire and reflect on what is most important to you, without distraction.

Knowing what your values, non-negotiables, likes and dislikes are, really help to build a solid sense of self, which in turn makes you feel safe and secure. When you have been used to following along with the wishes of others, creating space to really understand what is valid for you now is empowering.

Some examples of self-inquiry questions are:

- ♥ What makes my heart sing?
- ♥ What motivates me?
- ♥ Where would I like to visit?
- ♥ Do I like the gym, swimming or cycling? Or do you prefer Yoga, Tai Chi or Karate?
- ♥ What foods do I really like?

Create space for the truth

Creating space gives other people the chance to either notice your absence and reconnect or choose not to. Although this can be triggering, it will give you valuable information. You may feel like I did at first; that I was abandoning my ex-husband. Remember though that being in your own space is a really safe place to be. Pausing and not diving in to fix becomes easier the more you practice. Holding back whilst respecting your own boundaries and needs first is self-love and compassion in action.

Give yourself space, let them do what they're going to do, and prioritise accordingly. It can be tough to wait — you may have to sit on your hands — however you deserve to surround yourself with people who want to be in your space with you. Being with people who are healthy and supportive is self-soothing as they are likely to feel calm to your nervous system i.e., feel safe and nurturing to be around.

By giving yourself some space to breathe, decompress and re-evaluate, you are discovering new aspects of yourself and your relationships which would have otherwise been hidden.

5. HO'OPONOPONO

Ho'oponopono is a Hawaiian forgiveness ritual that you can use if something is troubling you, you are upset or suffering and it doesn't seem to be going away; or if you feel betrayed or hurt and cannot shake it off. It is a wonderful method of healing.

Method

Focus on the person or problem and then repeat these words as a mantra as many times as you need to until you feel a shift. You may like to put one hand on your heart and one on your tummy or both hands on your heart whilst practicing Ho'oponopono.

Whilst practicing this mantra, tears may flow and a felt sense that your body and mind is relaxing may develop. The experience can be beautifully uplifting as you let go of heavy negative thoughts and energy and allow the space to be filled with love and gratitude.

Mantra

I am sorry

Please forgive me

I love you

Thank you

The practice of Ho'oponopono is based on taking self-responsibility for anything that affects your state of being and is a simple yet powerful method of healing. In Hawaiian, "ho'o" means "to cause" or "to make," and "pono" means "balance," "rightness," or "harmony." Together, "ho'oponopono" can be interpreted as "to make things right" or "to bring into balance." The practice teaches the importance of love and forgiveness through a process that allows you to release burdens, enabling deep healing.

Forgiveness is a skill that aids your recovery from the anger and distress of negative experiences. Saying these words helps you to navigate through tricky emotions. Practicing Ho'oponopono is an act of personal strength and courage where you can approach your future with a clean slate. It encourages and distils within you an openness to interactions without blame, shame or resentment.

Ho'oponopono encourages you to recognise that your core motivations, the energy you put out, affect what you attract towards you. Practicing the art of forgiveness and acceptance cleanses your heart and mind so that you can find contentment.

6. UNCONDITIONAL LOVE EXERCISE

Metta loving-kindness meditation

When you are going through something difficult, your fear or contraction can make you feel alone. Practicing compassion, and in particular loving-kindness, helps you to be a better friend to yourself; to adopt a gentler attitude towards yourself and create a feeling of calm and safety. Practicing this meditation can help you let yourself off the hook more often and bring some kindness towards yourself on both good and bad days.

During the loving-kindness meditation, you focus benevolent and loving energy toward yourself and others. It's a practice that reminds you that every living being, including yourself, wishes to live in peace and happiness.

The phrases need to be meaningful to you, heartfelt and profound; things that you would wish for yourself and wish for others. Here are some commonly used phrases that you can begin with, feel free to adapt them:

May I be peaceful

May I be safe

May I be happy

May I live with ease

May I be free from suffering

Sometimes — perhaps often, offering these phrases will seem very ordinary, dry or mechanical, but that's OK. It doesn't mean that nothing is happening or that it's not working. What's important is to do it, to practice saying the phrases. Form an intention to use them to relieve suffering. You are uniting the power of loving-kindness and the power of intention and that is what will produce the effect of free-flowing loving-kindness.

Guided loving-kindness meditation

To begin, sit in a comfortable position with your back upright. Close your eyes and bring your attention to your breath.

Find the phrases you would like to use to offer good wishes. Take a few deep breaths, relaxing the body. Repeat very gently the phrases that reflect what you wish most deeply for yourself. For example:

May I be peaceful

May I be healthy

May I be happy

May I live with ease

May I know love

It may help you to connect to the loving essence of the phrases by placing one or both hands on your heart as you bring them to mind.

Take a moment to truly feel and comprehend the meaning of each phrase. You can repeat a phrase more than once or you may choose a single word and repeat this to yourself. The main beauty of this practice is in the intention.

If you notice that your mind starts to wander, simply return your attention to these phrases. Remember it's normal to get distracted.

Before you complete your practice, you may like to offer the following phrases:

May I and all other beings be peaceful

May I and all other beings be healthy

May I and all other beings be happy

May I and all other beings know love

7. GROUNDING

Grounding is a practice of energetically connecting to the Earth's natural electric charge that steadies and heals you at the deepest levels. Practicing grounding reduces stress and generates greater well-being. Grounding is an effective way to calm anxiety.

It brings you back into your body instead of living up in your head, which may be swirling. It is a lovely way to self-soothe as it is relaxing and comforting to feel 'in your body'. It gives you a sense of security and safety, that you have all your wits and senses available to you. Being grounded means that you are confident and sure of yourself.

When you're grounded, you have a strong connection with who you are. You're in control of your mental and emotional self, and not easily influenced by other ideas or individuals. You allow life's small mishaps to roll off your shoulders. For example, if someone cuts you off in traffic, you may give a shoulder shrug, and think: "Oh well, they must be in a hurry." You won't become overwhelmed by, or reactive to, the incident.

Grounding — Connecting to the Earth

Grounding, at its root, is the practice of connecting to the Earth to soothe and heal you. You can imagine its effects like a plant growing from a stable and nourishing plot of land. It will stand taller and grow stronger if it is supported and nurtured by an unconditionally loving source. Simply taking your shoes and socks off and standing on the Earth to take some deep breaths is relaxing and nourishing. You can lie down on the Earth and feel the healing support, or you can use grounding techniques.

I find grounding extremely useful. When I was suffering the most in the early days and months after my breakup, I would often go outside, day or night, whether it was warm or cold, whip my socks off and stand on the grass. I could feel the tension, pain and grief draining from me into the ground as I took some deep breaths and let go. Sometimes I would also shake my arms and hands to release any stubborn pent-up energy. After standing for a few minutes — or sometimes longer — I always feel more self-assured, contented and calm.

8. LET GO

Letting go of someone or something is not an easy thing for most of us to do. Letting go can be scary as it means stepping into the unknown. Remember that as humans we an inherent aversion to uncertainty — the unknown can trigger feelings of fear, doubt and vulnerability which we want to avoid.

You may imagine or have thoughts of something ending up much worse than before, or of losing the thing forever. For example, you may think that you will never have the same depth of love, the quality of friendship, or the camaraderie as you had with this relationship, friendship or job.

If thoughts like this arise, I invite you to consider the phrases, "As one door closes another one opens", and *"What's for you won't pass you by"*

Of course, each relationship and situation are different, however this is not a negative thing. Each time you meet new people and have a variety of experiences, your world expands. Exposing yourself to novel people, activities and perceptions enables you to see through a new lens, creating opportunities for enhanced fun, fulfilment and personal growth.

Letting go and allowing what will be to unfold involves trust. If you have been betrayed or disappointed in the past, then rebuilding trust may be required. Making a conscious decision to let go of the past — to forgive yourself and others — can help to achieve this. Holding onto old negative memories takes up space, space that you could free up to enable fresh energy to blow into your life.

Leave exaggerated or negative thoughts behind, put down any worries or concerns and bring in gratitude for yourself and all the good things in your life. Let the love in that is all around you. This creates space for new opportunities for growth and manifestation.

Here's a useful reminder in the form of the acronym, LET GO:

Leave

Exaggerated or negative

Thoughts

Gratitude

Opportunities

9. FIND A LIGHTER THOUGHT TOOL

It had snowed in Northumberland overnight, a good sprinkling of that lovely light fluffy snow that's really white. The glorious bright sunshine we woke up to made the snow glisten and sparkle.

As I was feeling uplifted when Molly and I got into the car, I thought it would be fun to play with the snow a little. I opened the windows and watched as the snow that had been collected on the glass remained intact and stood to attention, suspended in mid-air for a moment. On closer inspection as the light streamed through the snow, the individual snowflakes came into focus with their beautiful intricate patterns; they were a lovely sight.

Then some of the snow folded in on itself and fell inside the car. I laughed, enjoying the moment. A little while before that however was a different story, a different mood. I had noticed myself getting caught up in some heavy thoughts. Thoughts of worry and concern about the future. I felt gravity was taking my chin closer to the floor and my head becoming like lead on my shoulders. As soon as I recognised what my body was doing, I immediately caught my train of thought.

As I am luckily well practiced in catching my thoughts, the moment I recognised I was beginning to be carried away by them and they were about to spiral negatively perhaps out of control, the sentence "find a lighter thought" popped into my awareness. It made me smile, I gave myself a self-compassionate inner hug and reached for a more positive dialogue. For a higher vibration.

My body straightened, my head lifted, my shoulders went back and down, and I felt happy once again.

Find a lighter thought tool

Take a moment to tune into your body and notice how it feels. Once you recognise there is a level of discomfort, take your mind back to what you were thinking. Notice any heavy thoughts and find a lighter thought instead. Reframe the negative into more of a positive, in other words think the opposite. It may take a few attempts to reach a lighter thought. Once you do find a lighter thought, tune in again to your body and you will likely notice that your whole being feels lighter.

Example:

Heavy thought train

"I've got so much to do, how am I going to fit it all in? I think I'm starting to get a cold; I hope it's not going to be too busy at work later."

Lighter thought train

"There's plenty of time to do everything I want to do. It's the weekend tomorrow. I really enjoy my work and the people are wonderful."

Lighter thoughts are encouraging, motivating and put you back to feeling in control. Negative and heavy thoughts are not very productive and can drag you down. If you are dragged down far enough you can start to believe that you have no control, no safety which can lead to stress and depression. Give yourself the gift of a lighter thought and catch that train.

PART 5

Paths to clarity

Chapter 18

ROLE MODELS

A young boy is happily playing in his garden on a bright sunny day. He squeals with glee as he runs rings around his brother playing tag. They climb their favourite tree as they have done many times before. Then there is a snap, a crack and a big thud. The branch has snapped and the boy falls from the tree, cutting his knee.

His mother, upon hearing the commotion, comes outside and sooths him. She shows him compassion and concern, gives him a cuddle, puts a plaster on his knee and lets him know he was OK.

The following week, the boy is playing football with his friend on the school field when his friend goes for a tackle and hurts his leg. He drops to the ground gripping his leg and shouting in pain.

The boy runs over to his friend and shows him kindness. He helps him up and then supports him as he hops off the field.

Sometime later, the boy fails his maths test. He tried his best, yet there were questions he just didn't know the answer to. Alone in his bedroom and feeling a bit sad about having to retake the test, he is compassionate towards himself. He offers soothing words of encouragement to himself.

He has learnt to internalise his role models' positive and nurturing responses and so is able to model that behaviour to his friend and himself. Unfortunately, this is not always the case. Not everyone grows up learning or having modelled to them care and compassion.

For example, when my husband left, the matriarch closed ranks. Not only did my children lose their dad, but they also essentially lost the whole side of his family. Birthday cards and Christmas wishes stopped. A complete shutout, seemingly encouraged by a grandmother. My heart broke into more pieces, not so much for me but for my children.

It made sense to me then why my husband behaved in the ways he did. Stonewalling, withholding, blaming and controlling were just some of the ways he conducted himself because that was all he knew to do.

As much as I attempted to show him a different way, his patterns were ingrained. I eventually realised that, as much as I loved him, it was a fruitless task attempting to alter his perceptions once his mind was made up. Whilst he had a choice to join me on a journey of personal growth, it was absolutely his right not to take up my invitation.

> *"The more you love someone, the more you touch their pain."*
>
> - Jeffrey Allen

In a relationship, you both bring to the surface the hurts that are underlying and available to heal. You each bring out these pains and wounds so that they can be recognised and explored. It's one of the beautiful gifts of being in a relationship, the chance to gently and compassionately show your loved one where their hurts are and give them the opportunity to work on those. It's your job to be kind and it's their job to choose whether they are willing to heal or not.

I discovered that the more I found love for myself and asked for what I wanted and needed, the quicker our relationship changed. The enhanced quality and depth of my love began to transform me and then radiated outwards. It was felt. It touched him. It was then a matter of choice for us as individuals what to do with this new level of awareness.

It intrigued me how these patterns came to be. I wanted to find out more, to understand, heal and learn so that I could be the best role model I could be for our children. Rather than getting bogged down in blame, judgement or feeling like a victim, I took the stance of the beginner's mind.

I remembered that I had learnt about attachment styles a few years before and they piqued my interest again. They offer a model of how we learn to be in relationships, and I was hopeful they would offer me some clarity. I immersed myself in the topic, pulled out my books on the subject and attended a few online courses. I had many lightbulb moments.

Chapter 19

ATTACHMENT STYLES — THE DANCE OF CONNECTION

Love and connection are extraordinarily important for human beings — you are hardwired for connection.

The dance of connection happens whenever you interact with others. The moment you are interacting with someone, their rules on how to relate with others will dance with yours. There is probably nothing that impacts you more than your attachment style when it comes to relationships.

Connection with others changes the way you see yourself, how you perceive others, and the way you view the world. Connection changes your physical well-being and impacts your level of life satisfaction and how much you love yourself. Your attachment style also has a major impact on how you feel about romantic relationships in general. It impacts the way you feel about commitment, closeness, connection and communication.

Knowing how to be in relationships is not automatic. Most likely you have not been taught directly what to look for in a secure partnership. That's OK. Bringing awareness to it now means that you will be more discerning about your patterns and those of your loved ones in future.

Your attachment style is essentially the set of rules you are subconsciously wired to play by when it comes to connecting with others, as a result of your childhood experiences of attachment and connection to your caregivers.

Like any other skill, being in a healthy, balanced and loving relationship takes knowledge and practice. Relationships can be very difficult when you have different attachment styles from the people you love, because you are playing the game of connection differently. Awareness of attachment styles can open a whole new way for you to approach relationships, starting with the most important one, the one you have with yourself.

There are three main attachment styles

Secure

Avoidant

Anxious

Secure Attachment is characterised by self-worth, self-reliance, emotional maturity, and honest communication.

Securely attached people enjoy intimacy and are comfortable with it. They are emotionally intelligent, understand emotions and show empathy. They hold the belief that the world is safe and predictable. They tend to provide emotional and practical support without withdrawing or playing any games. They give but also expect to get back.

Avoidant Attachment is characterised by someone avoiding vulnerability, closeness, and intimate attachment to others.

An avoidantly attached person may avoid relationships and crave independence; they don't value close relationships like the other styles do. They may be very social, easy-going, fun to be around and yet are happy to be alone. They tend to be steady, reliable, good problem solvers who get the job done.

Anxious Attachment is characterised by someone who is anxious in relationships and has low self-esteem.

They want to be close to others but are afraid that people don't want to be with them. They are very attuned to their partner's needs and sensitive to the relationship's needs.

Anxiously attached people tend to give a great amount and settle a lot to make relationships work. When they feel the relationship is threatened, they will attempt to control the situation.

An important note to remember is that attachment styles are not personal. They are learnt. The good news is, you can relearn and move towards a secure attachment style.

In the rest of this chapter, I am going look at these three attachment styles in depth and there are going to be some exercises that can help you to determine your attachment style.

TAKE FIVE PAUSE AND PRACTICE

Questions to ponder.

Give yourself a point for each answer below you say yes to:

- ♥ Do you ignore problems or pretend they are not happening?
- ♥ Do you believe that circumstances aren't that bad?
- ♥ Do you avoid asking for what you want and need?
- ♥ Do you stay in relationships where you have been betrayed? Where they have been untrustworthy? Where they have been rude to you? Disrespectful or cruel?
- ♥ Are you afraid of making mistakes or struggle to make decisions?
- ♥ Do you think deep down that you are not worthy enough, lovable enough?
- ♥ Do you end relationships too soon because you have an urge to be independent?
- ♥ Do you seek out approval or the thoughts of others rather than trusting yourself?
- ♥ Do you feel compelled to help people solve their problems?
- ♥ Do you anticipate other people's needs and wonder why they don't do the same for you?

If you answered:

1-3: You are generally self-aware and have a good sense of self-worth.

4-7: You may notice some patterns that don't fully support your well-being. This is a great chance to explore new ways to nurture yourself.

7-10: You're in the right place to start putting yourself at the centre of your Universe.

Did you say yes to all these questions, or perhaps a few in particular?

The higher your score, the more likely it is that you would benefit from learning how to love and connect with yourself more. To move towards being securely attached and understanding what true love and intimacy can offer. Putting yourself first and remembering that you are the most important person in your world.

Oops, I forgot about me

I was having dinner with my lovely mum one night and we were talking about how many beings I have in my care. I remarked that I have 6; Oliver, Molly, Maya and Pepper our dogs and Maisie and Merlin our cats.

Mum looked at me with a quizzical look and said no there are seven. I counted again and then realised what she was saying. The seventh person is me! I completely discounted myself.

This realisation stopped me in my tracks and caused me to ponder. I was quite shocked and taken aback that I had not thought about myself. I felt a heaviness in my chest and a wave of despondence wash over me. How could I have forgotten about myself? The thought disturbed me. I said it out loud as a response to my exasperation: *How did I forget about myself?*

I consider myself as a person who likes herself, who is emotionally intelligent and thoughtful, yet I did not factor myself into the equation. This loving comment from my mum made me (figuratively) stand up and want to make a change. It encouraged me to remember that I am important and that I deserve to be nourished too.

It is an oversight that I'm sure mums, dads and partners the world over will recognise.

Remember please to take care of yourself first and foremost. Think of filling your cup up so that you can then nurture all the beings in your care from the overflow, rather than by parching yourself. You don't want to turn into a dried-up husk!

Ingredients of a healthy relationship

When I began to delve into the world of attachment styles, what really stood out to me were the ingredients needed to feel good about myself and others whilst in a relationship. The more I learnt about the different styles, the more parallels I could identify within myself and what had been out of balance in my marriage.

The checklists and tips for how to be securely attached gave me something to aim for. A guideline for where my growth areas were. This reassured me because I was concerned, as you may be, that I would fall into the same patterns again. I wanted to take the time to heal and develop as an individual before testing out my new way of being with someone new.

A reminder: it's when you are in a relationship with others that your patterns will emerge. That's where the learning and magic happen.

The goal of secure attachment

"I feel good about myself, and I feel good about other people."

Being securely attached does not mean that you are always confident. There may be some occasions when you have difficulty identifying or communicating your emotions. Or times when you aren't assertive or speak directly. Overall, however, you will be able to form healthy relationships, be comfortable on your own, and have the ability to manage your emotions.

Here's a checklist that you can mentally or physically tick off to let you know the areas where you are securely attached. It also serves as a guideline for personal growth areas.

Secure attachment checklist

- ♥ You can connect with yourself and others
- ♥ You can communicate well
- ♥ You have healthy boundaries
- ♥ You are OK in alone time
- ♥ You feel fundamentally safe
- ♥ You trust relationships
- ♥ You have appropriate and healthy boundaries
- ♥ You have a good self-esteem
- ♥ You do not shame yourself or others
- ♥ You have fulfilling and meaningful relationships
- ♥ You can be vulnerable and open in love.

I hope this checklist provides you with some insights and food for thought.

I invite you to journal on what you have learnt from these statements and how they made you feel.

The tortoise and the bull

There are two other very typical attachment styles many people fall into, either in family dynamics or in close romantic relationships. They are the avoidant and anxious attachment styles.

When you love someone, there is a general expectation that they will behave in kind and loving ways towards you no matter what. You may be accustomed to their thoughtful gestures, bids for connection and warm, reassuring hugs.

It is then a confusing, painful shock to the system when, during a time of upset or stress such as the threat of divorce or the loss of a job, they behave in ways that are alien to you. At a time when you would perhaps benefit the most from support and compassion, on the face of it, they are unavailable to you.

Times of stress and trauma can bring out learnt coping mechanisms. When faced with these experiences you are likely to display an aspect of one out of two different strategies, either to withdraw or confront. In many relationships one partner will be a "tortoise" and the other a "bull".

This dynamic can help both people to recognise their patterns and to seek to heal them. To dance towards secure attachment. Unfortunately, as relationships like babies don't come with manuals, attachment styles and their effect on relationships are not widely known, and so many of us don't recognise the dance or the steps.

The tortoise

If you are the tortoise, when triggered, your coping response will be to go into your shell, hide and withdraw. You may say things that dismiss other people's feelings, brush them off and invalidate them.

Saying things like:

"What's the big deal?"

"I'm sorry you feel that way."

"You shouldn't feel that way."

"Don't think about it, just get on with it."

"I'm not having this discussion!"

These kinds of words and actions are very painful for the bull in particular.

Attempting to hide from the pain and not wanting to feel it can cause unnecessary anguish to you and those close to you. Hiding from the pain and stuffing it down is a temporary fix. Those emotions are stored in your body and, if not let out, felt and healed, they will come out in bursts of frustration and anger at unpredictable times.

When you attempt not to feel pain, you also cheat yourself out of feeling love and joy.

> *"We cannot selectively numb emotions, when we numb the painful emotions, we also numb the positive emotions."*
>
> - Brene Brown

The bull

If you are a bull, your coping mechanism when triggered is to confront and to chase validation. You may say things in an attempt to have your emotions respected or to test someone's reaction.

Things you may say or do:

"I want to discuss this right now."

Exaggerate to gain sympathy.

Overreact and go on the attack.

Slam doors and shout.

Bring up past hurt not relating to the issue.

These kinds of words and behaviour can feel very confrontational to a tortoise. The result of this is that the tortoise will retreat more, and the bull will charge towards them more.

The bull in you is essentially frightened and anxious, so you attempt to confront as a coping mechanism to seem strong and in control. You don't want to feel vulnerable or anxious.

Healthy ways to reduce the charge and drama are to find ways to meet your own needs, to self-soothe and to accept that vulnerability is a superpower. Being aware of which strategy you adopt — i.e.; tortoise or bull — can help you to move away from painful ways of coping in difficult situations and towards more helpful ways of self-regulation and self-soothing.

Let me now take you deeper into the characteristics of the tortoise and the bull. Understanding where these behaviours, thoughts and feelings came from can be validating and an aid to healing and growth.

Avoidant attachment style: The tortoise

This attachment style occurs when there has been prolonged emotional neglect. This neglect can sometimes be overlooked because the child's physical and intellectual needs are met, whilst the emotional needs are not. It's very common for the avoidant to be unaware that something is missing because they perceive themselves to have had a good childhood.

Some of the core wounds of the avoidant include: "I am defective, I am bad, I am unsafe, I am trapped."

A person with an avoidant attachment is usually a gentle person who is fearful of connection and confused about love, therefore is emotionally unavailable to themselves and others. They didn't have anyone to mirror their emotions or how they were feeling inside, to understand and hear them, and so they had to rely on themselves. This over-focus on themselves is a reaction to earlier disappointments at being let down. They expect to be hurt or that no one will be there for them when they reach out for connection.

The avoidant often fears being smothered or invaded in romantic relationships. This makes them feel trapped and powerless. In their perception if they give too much or get too close then their resources will be stolen or taken away, including shared aspects of themselves.

This leads to using a survival strategy of tending to take more than they give, they are focused on hoarding what they have to stay afloat and alive. They have a high need for security and their home is likely to be a sanctuary or safe haven.

Please remember that this is not personal, it's a symptom of their nervous system being in flight or fight mode. It is happening often outside of conscious awareness or choice, until it is intentionally brought to the surface to be explored and healed.

Abandonment/ dismissive

Abandonment is a fear of the avoidant.

They assume that they will be abandoned at some point and so they build positive associations to being alone. They keep their space and distance as alone time gives them a sense of relief. They have a pattern of dismissing other people's feelings, thoughts or ideas as another way of maintaining a level of disconnection, so they avoid the pain of being hurt.

Anxiety

When there is a lot of fear-based thinking happening, it affects the nervous system. Thoughts like "*I am not good enough*", "*something is wrong with me*" and a sensitivity to criticism can mean that a person can spend a lot of time in fight, flight, freeze mode. With a background feeling of nervousness or anxiety, they have a hard time sitting still. Choosing to immerse themselves in doing something and losing themselves in it inadvertently reinforces abandoning their emotional self.

Emotions

Emotions are seen as bad or feared to be unsafe. Vulnerability is viewed as unsafe. This person believes that conflict is bad and can signal the end of a relationship when, in fact, it is a healthy part of a relationship. In conflict they will try and escape, deflect and run away. Emotions are feared because the person has not learnt how to access and regulate them. Therefore, the use of disagreements to make space, or to clear the air is frightening.

Decisions

People with an avoidant pattern can be indecisive. All decisions are emotionally based, so making decisions can be hard because they find it tough to access emotions.

When you are disconnected from your emotions, it can be hard to be clear about your decisions. Your emotions are a guiding light and when that light is dimmed it can be difficult to see where to go.

Later in life, especially during times of change or when an important decision needs to be made, these people become attached to their parent or parents' approval. This is due to having a small amount of emotional connection with them which is amplified. They can care very deeply about what their parents think and will make decisions to make them happy.

They can feel unheard and misunderstood because they are absorbing other people's emotions and not hearing or connecting with theirs. It takes quite some time for them to be able to process their emotions and to speak up for what they want and need.

Flaws

Avoidant people in a romantic relationship tend to focus on their partner's flaws. Noticing little details and using them as justifications for nitpicking and keeping partners at arms' length or pushing them away. This helps them to feel safe by not allowing themselves to get too close as they believe that truly committing and being vulnerable is not safe.

Rather than attempting to solve the issues in the relationship, finding faults and flaws feels more comfortable. Especially with underlying beliefs like "this will never work anyway", "this person is too emotional", "this is going to end", or "the person will leave anyway so I should just push them away now".

The avoidant's lesson is to learn how to be dependent, close and connected without feeling overly vulnerable.

Anxious attachment style: The bull

This attachment style tends to come from a childhood where the parents were on then off; very inconsistent with their time and balance of emotions. Leaving the child trying to figure out when they could connect and when they could not connect to the parent. Parents may have been very busy and focused elsewhere, unavailable or unaware of the child's present needs. The parents may have been emotionally volatile and shouted a lot, and/or emotionally passive and easy-going, therefore not offering a sense of grounding or stability.

This can leave the child feeling like the other person is a moving target, never quite sure when they can connect.

The child then starts to think: "*Is it me? Am I not lovable enough?*"

These beliefs feed a lack of self-esteem and the person will put a lot of energy into proving themselves worthy of love and attention as they try to prove themselves to be the 'right' person in a relationship.

Attuning to the needs of the partner or other person instead of or before their own needs becomes the norm, which can be exhausting. Being outwardly focused rather than inwardly focused means a lack of attention paid to themselves. Emotional bankruptcy and even resentment can build due to being unable to articulate their own needs.

People with a pattern towards fear and anxiety respond to their confusion around connection by being hyper-alert to any cues. These cues can be misconstrued and interpreted negatively, leading to deep hurt.

People with an anxious tendency need to find ways to self-soothe and self-regulate.

Complaining

Sometimes the anxious person will attempt to get their needs met by complaining. Their bids for support may sound demanding or attacking which can be off-putting to the person on the receiving end.

Complaining is likely to be a last resort for the anxious person who has attempted to express their needs without being appropriately answered. They may have asked for what they wanted or needed in a way they hoped would get them the response they required, yet it did not. Therefore, if the requirement is still present, the anxious person will up the ante to complaining.

They aren't choosing to be negative, it's part of what has been wired into their nervous system, like a signal cry from a baby. Babies cry to express their needs and emotions, when they have had enough of something, they will have a fussy, whiny cry.

Old wounds

It is hard for anxiously attached people to heal old wounds, and they tend to hold onto hurts for a long time. They dredge up old stuff when they are triggered and say things like:

"You did this thing three years ago so why should I...", then use this as a starting point to bring up everything else that they are unhappy about.

The anxious person's lesson is to learn how to be more independent whilst communicating their needs affectively. The more you do for yourself, the more choice, stability and support you can receive.

"Love holds no records of wrongs" is a powerful statement to consider when learning to heal this attachment style.

Rejection

Anxiously attached people enjoy connection and meaningful relationships and, therefore, fear rejection. They tend to dislike being out of a relationship and so will go to great lengths to hold onto or remain in a relationship. They may offer the other person time and space to consider things carefully. They might suggest counselling or other forms of reconnection like more date nights.

An anxiously attached person may feel that they are not adequate or lovable enough for another relationship. They may cling to one that is not healthy for them fearing that no other relationship will be as good.

Approval

The anxiously attached person can put other people on pedestals, believing that other people are better than or superior to them. This can lead to people pleasing and putting their needs aside to win the approval of others.

This is a survival strategy which comes from the times we were hunter-gatherers; the Neanderthals. In those times, if you were ostracised or cast out of the community for some reason you would not survive — the conditions were too harsh. It was much safer to be part of a tribe. Therefore, because you still have the ancient part of your brain — the limbic brain — you equate approval with survival.

TAKE FIVE PAUSE AND PRACTICE

Now that you have a flavour of the secure, avoidant and anxious attachment styles, I invite you to look at the questions below with a new lens.

Do any of the questions jump out at you? Perhaps give you a jolt?

If so, I invite you to get quiet and comfortable. To listen to your thoughts and tune into your feelings and journal on your discoveries.

Questions to ask yourself

- Is/ was this relationship for you?
- Are your boundaries honoured and respected?
- Do you trust yourself or do you question yourself in this relationship?
- Are your needs being met in the relationship?
- When you express your needs are you shamed, or do they do their best to accommodate them?
- Are they able to ask for their needs to be met? And can you meet them?
- Is the relationship safe? Are they protective (not overly)?
- Are they interested, connected and engaged in what you say and do?

Love allows, honours, and appreciates; attachment grasps, demands, needs, and aims to possess.

Chapter 20

CREATE YOUR FIRST AID KIT

I invite you to take a journey through your senses and create a kit to support you on your most vulnerable days. You know those days when you need to be alone, snuggled up with a box of tissues and chocolate because you are exhausted, confused, upset and need to recharge and recover?

Before I explain further, let me tell you a little story.

Driving to my beautiful friend Lizzie's house not long after my break-up, I found myself on a gorgeous country road bathed in sunshine, but was consumed with sorrow and needing a big hug. As I approached a crossroad, a white flatbed builders' van turned the corner sharply and a large toolbox flew off the side, slid across the road and stopped to kiss my bumper.

I was taken aback at first, quite bemused at this unusual experience. I put my hazard lights on, got out of the car and waved at the van, hoping to catch the driver's attention as they disappeared up the road oblivious to their lighter load. So I hauled this heavy box to the grass verge and rescued a screwdriver, tape and hammer that had been strewn across the road.

As I carried on my way, I had a strong sense that what had just happened was a sign from Life. A lovely warm wave of love and support washed over me as I realised that the toolbox was a gift. It had been sent across my path to let me know that I had all the tools I needed to get through this life remodel. This gave me such a lift and I thought about over often in the coming weeks; a reminder whenever I got overwhelmed or felt alone.

First aid kit ideas: Using the five elements to heal and soothe

Below are some ideas to get you started. The first aid kit can be a mixture of physical items, emotional supports, smells, foods and sounds. If you'd like to get creative, you could find yourself a lovely box, fill it with the physical items, a journal and pen plus notes on your favourite soothing aids.

Feel free to give any of the suggestions a go and practice the ones that soothe you the most.

Wood

If your birth star is 3 or 4 Tree:

- ♥ Name five things that you see around you that make you happy.
- ♥ Surround yourself with soothing colours like green, dark blue and indigo.
- ♥ Assess your anger on a scale of 1-5 (five being the highest)
- ♥ Look at reminders of your success: certificates, emails and thank you notes, for example.

Fire

If your birth star is 9 Fire:

- ♥ Eat something nourishing.
- ♥ Share a story with someone.
- ♥ Think about three people in your life who have your back and love you unconditionally.
- ♥ Ask a loved one for a hug.

Earth

If your birth star is 2,5,8 Earth:

- ♥ Choose one small thing to organise like a drawer or shelf.
- ♥ Do a simple breathing technique such as box breath: breathing in for four counts, hold for four and breathe out slowly for four counts.
- ♥ Remember particular times that you have helped someone in the past.
- ♥ Use aromatherapy oils such as bergamot, clove, rosewood.

Metal

If your birth star is 6, 7 Metal:

- ♥ Listen to some calming music.
- ♥ Get quiet, pause and rest.
- ♥ Go for a slow quiet walk around the block.
- ♥ Journal for a few minutes about the emotions and details surrounding the stressful situation

You can also go back through this book and note down any of the self-soothing tools that resonated with you.

The staples in my kit are Bach's Rescue Remedy, a rose quartz heart, chocolate, and a soothing meditation. My absolute favourite is adding warmth by either using a heated wheat bag or putting my hands on my heart, breathing deeply and allowing myself to relax.

Go gently with yourself and remember that self-soothing, rest and recovery are paramount to your well-being.

My first aid kit checklist

- ✢ _____
- ✢ _____
- ✢ _____
- ✢ _____
- ✢ _____
- ✢ _____

Chapter 21

A HORSE CALLED WENDY

Being in nature is restorative. It helps you to be present by offering a feast for your five senses; sight, hearing, taste, smell and touch. Nature offers interesting sounds, smells and textures to explore. Whilst walking along if you intend to notice what you are experiencing, you will find that there is so much going on.

One of my favourite places to go is the woods, ideally with a stream or river. Whilst I am walking, I will bring my attention to a range of things one at a time. I may notice what kind of surface I'm walking on and how it feels or sounds. The hard gravel path that winds its way into the woods and transforms into a firm and sometimes claggy earthen base. The sound of scraping from the small stones of gravel underfoot compared to the wonderful sound your shoe makes when it's made a vacuum with the mud and your foot releases with a pop and a squelch.

Listening to the birds singing, the wind rustling the leaves on the trees, twigs snapping, water flowing, people chatting and dogs barking.

On a walk one day with Molly, rather than going our usual route and sitting on our favourite meditation bench, I suggested walking next to the river. I felt like water was calling me to listen, to go with the flow, and to let go of anything that needed to be released.

We stood on a wooden bridge, the sun warming our faces. I closed my eyes and listened to the water swirling, trickling and running under our feet at a fairly fast pace. The powerful and yet at the same time peaceful din was occurring beneath us, in front and behind us.

I opened my eyes and a flash of white caught my eye. In the distance walking up the hill in a kind of zig zag, somewhat unpredictable formation was a horse and its rider. The horse who. from that angle, looked quite large and muscular like a Shire Horse, was picking the route gingerly as though not to slip. Something told me that this horse and rider were not completely relaxed.

We watched as the horse meandered the twisting path towards us, and upon seeing the water, reared up onto her back legs whilst her rider calmly held on. The horse, who we could now see was quite young, stood well away from the water's edge and seemed to have no interest at all in crossing.

"Come on Wendy, you can do it," said the rider.

Wendy didn't budge an inch.

The rider looked over to us and explained that the horse had frightened her young, eight-year-old owner by rearing up and so she had been tasked with de-sensitising and socialising Wendy. Wendy was beautiful; black and white with a long fluffy mane and tail and sporting feathers on her legs, a Mini Gypsy Vanner breed.

This splendid symbol of power and strength — the kind of strength that can carry you forward — wearing the colours of balance, was anxious.

Wendy's rider was the epitome of calm and compassion, she knew that

Wendy could cross this unknown body of muddy water and gently coaxed her. It was a dance of one hoof forward and two hooves back. Whenever Wendy would attempt to reverse or retreat, her guide softly told her it was OK and that they were not going back. Wendy tentatively moved forwards a small amount at a time, eating an occasional blade of grass.

"Have a sniff of the water Wendy. You know what it is and you'll like it when you get in," said her rider, encouraging her to put one foot in.

As Wendy splashed the feathers on the bottom of her front hooves at the very edge of the stream, Molly and I dismounted the bridge and went to the other side to support and cheerlead.

"Come on Wendy, you can do it," we all said enthusiastically while her rider made lovely warm cooing type sounds as a form of encouragement.

After a few minutes of false starts, Wendy raised her head and slowly made her way across.

"Yay! Well done Wendy!" Molly and I cheered and clapped as this beautiful little horse overcame her fear and slowly trod up the woodland path.

The take aways I got from this encounter were many, including:

💛 I trusted my intuition, the inner nudge that said "This way" as we took a different route.

Nudges come to me in the form of a loving and secure voice that feels safe. Even if I have a moment of doubt, when I receive a thought that pops into my head as a timely and gently directive, I have learnt to trust it and follow its guidance. It often takes me down a path that I haven't explored before, metaphorically or physically.

These redirects or nudges always lead to something worth learning or exploring, which is why I trust them. If I hadn't listened to the nudge, we wouldn't have had such a lovely experience with Wendy and her rider and, indeed, I wouldn't have been able to share the story and my learnings with you.

You always have the answers within you, they are whispered and mirrored back to you through thoughts, feelings, intuition and deep knowings. Even when, in your heart of hearts, you know the truth of a situation, it can be hard or even painful to accept and allow. To listen rather than resist. Although it can be scary, if you allow it, life can show you new paths that will greatly exceed your expectations and take you to higher heights of happiness and contentment.

♥ Wendy couldn't see the bottom of the water and yet trusted that she would be OK

In life you don't always know what is at the top of the staircase or round the corner and, in order to know, you need to take steps one at a time. The more steps you take, the more information you have. The more you learn to trust that life is for you and loves you, the deeper your trust will be.

Wendy's ability to walk into unknown waters was aided by a few factors. She had experienced water before; she had built up some trust with her rider and she had an innate sense of her natural qualities.

Gypsy Vanners were originally bred to pull caravans and are impressive cart horses. Due to their strength and calm, mild-mannered characters, they can turn their hands to a range of purposes from competing in dressage shows to pulling carriages for pleasure.

Wendy, who — just like an acorn — is designed to grow into a mighty oak, naturally followed her inner design and used her strength and calm to take her rider across the river. Despite her initial reluctance she drew upon her skills and, with the encouragement of her guide, who reminded Wendy of her own natural calmness, conquered the river.

You won't always be able to see what you are walking into in life. Trust yourself and surround yourself with people who are grounded and supportive. Move through the fear to travel through the murk into crystal clear waters. Give yourself the opportunity to experience the wonders that await you on the other side of the unknown. Step in.

♥ Although Wendy wanted to go back, she persisted and went forward through the unknown waters.

I imagine there have been times in your life, as there have been in mine, where you wish you could go back to how it was before. Where it seemed safer, more secure and perhaps happier. Whilst it is lovely to reminisce, the past is behind you and the future is calling you forward.

You have a choice in the present moment to take what you have learnt from the past and either put things down or take them with you. Even a cart horse can only carry so much before the weight becomes too much.

I encourage you to put down the heavy weights of regret, remorse and resentment. To lighten your load and step forwards. To avoid the temptation to go back to what was and explore what is out there for you now.

Moving forwards takes courage, strength and persistence. Determination grows like a passionate spark that ignites within you and fuels the fire. The spark is unique to you. It may be the excitement that grows when you think about a more empowered, assertive version of you and how your life can be enriched by this new way of being.

It could be the feeling that opens your heart wide open when you imagine a new healthy relationship that offers true love, deep connection and is secure.

Whatever your spark of intention is, use it at times when you feel yourself wanting to shrink and go back. Those moments when your boundaries are being tested, your resolve is wavering and remember that the best way out is through or, as Thich Nhat Hahn says: *"The best way out is in"*, meaning go inwards to discover the answers to your quandaries.

♥ She was a symbol of strength and balance

Wendy epitomised strength with her strong, muscular build and the ability to transport a person on her back, her rider's weight evenly balanced to help carry the load. Even though Wendy was outwardly strong, she still needed to draw upon her inner strength to overcome her anxiety about crossing the river.

You are stronger than you think you are, I promise. As the Japanese proverb states, fall down seven times and stand up eight. Choose to never give up hope and always follow your dreams. Focus on what you can do rather than what you have no control over.

Until you are in a situation, you never really know how strong you can be, for yourself and for your family. I certainly surprised myself about how much strength I could muster to do the hard things I had to do. Days when I didn't want to face the world or leave the house yet still found the courage to go to the shops, make the difficult phone calls, and hold my children in their despair. All without crumbling or hardening.

I balanced my strength and courage with nurturing and compassion. I allowed myself days to cry and grieve, to miss and wonder. To hold myself with compassion as I berated myself for shoulda, coulda, woulda's that eventually morphed into acceptance, gratitude and peace.

Other days I was a tower of strength, with only little hints on the outside of the pain I was in and the experience I was enduring as I put my best foot forward and stepped into unknown territory.

One of the biggest things I had to do was swallow my pride and ask for government assistance. I had to be strong and at the same time balance that with being vulnerable. Having worked as a professional Careers Adviser for over a decade until 2014, being on the other side of the desk felt completely demoralising. I had the grace to know though, that the lovely lady across from me was there to help, and I was extremely grateful for the support afforded to me.

♥ Her rider showed her love, patience, compassion and softly supported her.

When your system is in overdrive from anxiety, fear and anguish, soothing is the best way to help you move forwards. Self-soothing or soothing offered by someone else enables you to relax, let go and put things into perspective.

Love can be shown in so many ways, from a gentle squeeze of the hand to being accompanied to something daunting, and someone making dinner for you. Love is like a warm comfort blanket that holds you close and enables you to soften.

Patience involves taking the time and not rushing; tolerating something that may take a while to complete. Wendy's rider took all the time she needed to cross the stream. She didn't get frustrated or annoyed, rather gently encouraged and persisted.

In times of change, a huge dollop of patience is likely to be required. There were many times when I had to dig deep into my reserves of patience as I healed and grew as a person. The times when I wanted to go ahead with moving on with my life and was thwarted by circumstances, grief and other people's actions.

Compassion is being sensitive to the emotional suffering of yourself and others. It is recognising that a certain amount of gentleness and help will make a difference to the suffering involved. To help in a constructive way.

Wendy's rider showed compassion to her steed by exposing her safely and slowly to new experiences that she anticipated Wendy would come across in the future. She was aware of her background and purpose, and wanted her to succeed. She knew the best way to do that was to support her through the challenges likely to be faced so that in similar situations Wendy would feel more confident and access her inner reserves where necessary.

♥ Her rider reassured her and offered words of affirmation.

Words are powerful and when coupled with the intonation and intention behind them, they are magic. Affirmations are statements designed to uplift, empower and brighten your outlook. They are positive, inspiring and often action orientated.

Examples are:

- ♥ I embrace the rhythm of life and let it unfold.
- ♥ I take steps to create the life I want.
- ♥ I know my intuition will always lead me in the right direction.
- ♥ I can become anything I put my mind to.

Wendy may not have known what the words meant and yet Wendy visibly relaxed more and more when her rider stroked her, talked to her and gave her little loving nudges. She continued to reassure Wendy until she felt confident to put her feet into the water. Her tone was upbeat and encouraging, there wasn't a hint of anger or despondence.

I know I respond better when I speak to myself or am spoken to with respect, honesty and kindness. When I am encouraged and built up I feel motivated to act, take a risk or help in some way.

Imagine if Wendy's rider took the opposite approach and berated her, shouted at her and put her down. The little horse would remain in her threat system and perhaps be even more anxious and skittish than she was before, thus serving no one.

On the days when your inner critic rears its head and you get frustrated or mad at yourself, remember please that in every moment you can begin again. Reach for gentle ways to talk to yourself in difficult moments. You can even go back to something you have said and restate it using new words from a more enlightened perspective.

♥ Nature and life offer lessons wherever we are willing to take a moment to notice.

Life is always talking to you.

I believe that if you open your heart and mind up to the possibility that there are lessons and signs being offered to you daily that your life can be richer. Taking notice of what is happening around you and what you are feeling can give you clues as to whether you are in alignment to your true self or not. Being in alignment offers more opportunities to live your best life, utilising your strengths and not being held back by challenging circumstances, thoughts or beliefs. To have an underlying sense that all is well and that you have the tools and support to overcome any trials.

Watching and interacting with Wendy and her rider gave me an abundance of beautiful lessons in just 25 minutes. Life is full of these experiences if you choose it to be so.

I watched a programme about a scheme in Africa where researchers and conservationists were designing inexpensive and easy to use devices to help keep elephants and humans who were living in the same area safe.

The researchers used the power of nature to help them come up with some ingenious ideas, as well as using their knowledge of what elephants do and don't like. They discovered that elephants are repelled by the sound of bees as they hate being stung, so they installed real and electronic beehives around the villagers' crops to keep everyone involved safe. The plus side also being that the villagers now had honey to eat and sell.

They also observed that the elephants dug up a particular root to quench their thirst when water was in short supply, so the villagers used the roots to feed and save their animals during droughts. These observations enabled the humans to grow their crops and live safely without them being trampled on. Now that the elephants were no longer a threat, the villagers could relax and observe their natural ways to sustain themselves. A wonderful example of nature offering lessons for peaceful living.

This programme reminded me of and validated my approach to life since my separation: that you don't have to use negative, unloving or cruel tactics to get what you want. You can use your natural resources, guided by love to keep everyone safe and away from harm. It was a reminder that boundaries are necessary to uphold peace and that kindness, respect and love create a harmonious environment.

THE THREE GIFTS

From the experience with a little horse called Wendy, I formulated the three gifts; presence, experience and sharing:

First gift: Presence

Being present and mindful; noticing what is around you, and really taking the time to slow down and be aware is a real gift. When you are in the present moment, you are in your power. You can focus on what you have control over right now, including your thoughts and actions. The past is behind you and the future is yet to come, so concentrating on the present can help you feel confident, content and calm.

Second Gift: Experience

Once you are in the present moment, your experience can be fully appreciated in full technicolour instead of black, white and grey. Experiences can be missed or fly past you if you skip the first gift of presence. Not all experiences will be pleasant — some may be painful — however they are still a gift and an opportunity for growth. Perhaps to stretch your comfort zone, to release you from being stuck, to give you insights about yourself or a situation.

Third gift: Sharing

Sharing connects you to others. It gives you insights and joy to recall and relay your experience. Hearing yourself talk or seeing your words on a page can highlight thoughts and feelings that have been playing in the background ready to be brought forward and illuminated. Equally, your story is likely to invoke the recipient's imagination too. You never really know the impact a story can have on someone else. It may remind them of a happy memory or offer the last piece to a puzzle through understanding a familiar concept through a new lens. A wonderful gift indeed.

Chapter 22

DRAINS AND RADIATORS

Your energy can be depleted by certain activities and filled up by others. Energy drains are activities or thoughts in daily life that drain your energy and lower your mood. Imagine your energy draining out of you, being sucked down a plug hole; that feeling of heaviness, apathy and exhaustion. You cannot live your purpose with too many energy drains.

Radiating activities are the ones where you feel joy, contentment and worth. The ones that fill you up and enable you to radiate or send out your positive energy, and know that it is appreciated and acknowledged.

For example, if someone calls and asks you to do something, I invite you to pay attention to what your mind and body does. If it is a likely energy drain you will feel a sinking, heavy feeling accompanied by unenthusiastic thoughts.

If someone else calls you and asks you to do something and your chest raises with a light feeling accompanied by enthusiastic thoughts, this is a great sign it will be a positive experience that radiates energy.

Not everything you are required to do in life is pleasurable. That said, your energy can give you clues as to who, what and when to use your precious energy.

If you are feeling particularly drained by an activity, where possible either limit the time you commit to it or wait until your energy is more balanced. It's always better to make choices and decisions from a neutral, centred and balanced place than from an overly negative or positive place. To utilise your energy efficiently to gain the best results.

One of the best decisions I made to lower my stress levels, to honour my energy and to take a burden off my shoulders was to have convenient, yummy and healthy food delivered weekly. Utilising a kit-based food delivery service has saved me hours of anguish over what meals to make and trips to the supermarket. We can sit and choose what we fancy to eat during the week and then sit back and relax. This is the Pareto Principle in action.

The Pareto Principle

The Pareto Principle or the 80/20 rule, suggests that using 20% of focused time on an activity produces 80% of the work. To identify and prioritise your best assets (in this case your energy) and use them efficiently to create maximum value.

You can use the 80/20 rule to prioritise the tasks that you need to get done during the day. The idea is that out of your entire task list, completing 20% of those tasks will result in 80% of the impact you can create for that day.

The tricky thing is that if you have been in an unbalanced relationship or work situation, you are probably used to giving away 80% of your energy and receiving 20%. This may be a revelation to you and so you will need to practice resetting the energy imbalance in your favour.

To do this, make a list of all the things that you need to get done today or this week. Then identify which tasks have the highest impact on your energy, quality of life and goals. Do any of your tasks result in a reduction of suffering; for example feeling reassured by talking to the bank about your finances, doing some exercise to relieve tension, or making a meal plan so that you feel organised?

It is also useful to consider when in the day your energy is at the highest to complete certain tasks. I know that my ideas flow in the morning and so I tend to write in the morning until early afternoon. I enjoy using my energy in this way as it feels like the words flow onto the page easily. If I attempt to accomplish the same amount of writing later in the afternoon or evening I find it takes me longer and the flow is lacking. Attempting to write despite my diminished energy could easily affect the quality of my words and my overall enjoyment of being creative.

TAKE FIVE PAUSE AND JOURNAL

Draw two columns on a blank piece of paper and title one side drains and the other radiators. Consider and feel into what activities you do or are upcoming that deplete your energy and the ones that nurture and enhance your energy. Aim to write at least 20 activities that you enjoy doing from simple to more involved.

Write the activities on the appropriate column.

From the drain column consider what activities you could prioritise and transform to make your life a bit easier and to recoup your energy. You may not be able to avoid some of the draining activities so think about how you can change how you engage with them.

For example, you could have a go at one of the following options:

- Get the activity done first thing in the morning or straight away so that you are not anticipating it all day.
- Break it up into bite-sized chunks and intersperse your time with enjoyable activities.
- Contemplate the benefits of completing the task so it becomes purposeful.

Be creative in ensuring that you do at least three things from the radiate column throughout your day. Add to your column with new radiating activities as often as you can.

Activities are not the only things that can affect your energy, people can too. In times of trauma, loss and grief you certainly find out who your friends are. Who you choose to spend time with or listen to during these difficult times will be a critical factor in how well you cope, personally and professionally.

People who truly care for you tend to find ways to support and help. From a little note on a text, bringing you chocolate and a hug, to holding and reflecting your dreams and desires.

In my experience the people who can see your strengths, courage and skills, and remind you of them when needed, are true friends and good eggs. A quote that I love by Arne Garborg sums it up nicely:

"To love someone is to learn the song in their heart and sing it back to them when they have forgotten."

Rise and shine or sayonara

Surround yourself with people who lift you up rather than pull you down. Release yourself from the cycle of self-blame. A part of self-love is having high standards when it comes to who you spend time with, and the people in your inner circle. Spending time with and listening to supportive, loving and grounded friends is healthy and healing. Connect with people who hold space for you and cause you to think, gain clarity, and see your world in new ways. This is what self-growth is all about.

During the process of my separation, good friends of mine suggested concepts that I originally squirmed at, and that made me sit up, take notice and consider. Sometimes I would be in resistance mode or confused by what they said. As I sat with the mixed feelings and allowed them to flow, new streams of thought emerged. That's the beauty of being with other people and not isolating yourself. You are exposed to new concepts, perceptions, energies and ideas that help you to rise and shine.

When you have been in a controlling, toxic or one-sided relationship, especially for a long time, it can be confusing to spend time with people who truly care. You may pinch yourself to make sure this level of empathy and respect is real and that you are worthy of it. When you have clipped your own wings, censored yourself, and have not been able to be your best self for a long time, it can feel strange to receive positive attention.

I made some mistakes when it came to who I got my advice from early on in my separation. There are courses online that are designed to help you rekindle and attract your wayward partner, that pull you in and sell you hope and false promises. Perfect for us empathic, rescuer-type folks. In my experience, what you actually get from these kinds of courses is more confusion, a greater sense of hopelessness, and feeling like a failure when the magic pill they offer doesn't work like a charm. These courses are damaging as they encourage self-criticism and forms of control instead of acceptance, compassion and love.

Following unhealthy relationships, it is common to experience confusion, self-blame, self-doubt, and anger. To stay up in your head, which stops you from being present and empathic — mainly towards yourself — until you become aware of the fact that you are loveable. That you are still and always will be a kind, loving and compassionate person, you may be inadvertently drawn towards the old you and the beliefs that go with that way of perceiving yourself and your life. The version of you that thinks you are responsible for the demise in your relationship, compounded and encouraged by another person telling you that you are to blame.

Let me remind you that it's your beautiful empathy, your true emotional connection and your self-reflective nature that leads you to blame yourself cruelly and unnecessarily. That clouds you from clearly seeing the harm that toxic people in your life are doing.

If this realisation stirs up anger in you, great! It's a healthy response to the manipulation, invalidation and sidelining you may have endured. If being an angry person is not how you want to move through the world, you can now choose to be loving, kind and compassionate instead.

The saying "birds of a feather stick together" can be very true and so, if you find yourself with negative people who blame or do not practice self-responsibility, then it's time to say "sayonara" and say yes to people who encourage you to rise and shine.

Stop listening to other people's blame or negativity and using the old cycles of self-blame to navigate by. Turn it into white noise in your head. Give yourself the gift of tuning into your truth and trusting who you are.

Chapter 23

CIRCLING BACK TO BOUNDARIES

Boundaries are like picket fences around the things you hold dear, special and sacred, such as your freedom and contentment. They are not solid walls that keep people out, they are a reminder of your space. Boundaries help you to be clear about where you end and someone else begins. I like to think of my boundary as a beautiful garden; a place that feels peaceful and safe to be in. The picket fence is a designated outer border that lets everyone know the line. If it wasn't there, then the garden is in danger of getting trampled on and peace disturbed.

Upholding loving and compassionate boundaries enables you to assert your sovereignty in a way that others can respect. They feel the truth of them and don't argue or push against them (at least when they are used to them). If you haven't had or upheld boundaries for a while it may take some people time to adjust, and there may be some resistance. Resistance to boundaries can come in the shape of anger, full-blown temper tantrums, frustration, begging or even sweet talking.

If you have been inadvertently training people to abuse or circumnavigate your boundaries, you can begin again and start asserting them today. People very quickly get used to what you will and will not tolerate. Having loose or non-existent boundaries gives others the green light to continue any behaviours that you do not call out.

If you are fearing backlash or saying yes to be nice, avoid being uncomfortable or in pain, shying away from stating a boundary is likely to inflame the situation and lead to resentment. Boundaries are kind. People who are healthy for you will not be put off by your boundaries, rather they will respect them.

Boundaries are an act of love; an act of compassion and empathy.

Putting your foot down and saying no enables you to be compassionate to yourself and others when they attempt to take advantage of you. "No" is a complete sentence. Honouring how you feel and allowing your truth to be the boundary is powerful and freeing. If something does not feel good to you, if you have a sense that the relationship is out of balance, or if the situation is not likely to be reciprocal, then you can confidently say no.

Boundaries are there to protect your integrity. They help you to grow and be more selective about where you use your energy. They can look after your wounds so that they don't get any worse. If you are or have been an over giver — someone who overcompensates or pours themselves out all the time, you will recognise the feeling of being exhausted, prone to martyrdom or resentment.

I know that does not feel good, especially when you come to realise that all the time you have been focusing on the other person, there has been deeper support available to you. Whilst you have been slogging away trying so hard to 'help' so that they are then in a better place to be with you and give you what you need, the solution was really to find a better balance with a boundary or to walk away.

Giving, serving, fixing, being nosey and getting into other people's lives when they have not asked for it can be smothering, hurtful and unhealthy. They are examples of boundary violations. Wha starts off as an idea to help or connect can, in reality, be more of a hinderance for the other person as they are best served discovering lessons for themselves.

If you tend to 'lean in' when others are telling you about their woes and difficulties; if you find yourself moving closer and closer, listening for how you can support, help or be of service, then lean back. Lean back and then find a neutral upright position to listen from. If you find yourself drifting forward, readjust.

Once you are solidly in your space, within your boundaries then you can be compassionate and empathetic. This does not mean, however, that you acquiesce to every request. It's better to breathe through the guilt of upholding boundaries than to betray yourself.

A useful way of teaching someone your boundaries is to state what is and is not OK with you and to express your feelings.

Here's an example from when Molly wanted her dad to come into the house and I wasn't ready yet.

I said:

"It's OK with me that you see him and spend time with him.

"It's not OK with me for you to invite him into our home when it still hurts to have him in my space."

Whilst I still had some kickback and pressure applied, I stuck to my guns because I knew and felt it was important to have empathy and self-compassion for my hurt and wounds.

It was also an opportunity for Molly and I to connect on a deeper emotional level, and for me to coach her on how to regulate her emotions of frustration and disappointment.

And just like that

I came across the new series of "Sex and the City" the other day. The programme was a staple of my weekly viewing back in the day! It was great to reconnect with Carrie, Miranda and Charlotte and observe how their lives had evolved over the last decades. How their relationships with their spouses, partners and children had changed. How they navigated a changing world and did their utmost to be good friends through chaotic, sad and confusing times.

Early in the series, Carrie's husband died suddenly. It was of course a big shock and a huge grief. Carrie also used writing as a tool to pour her emotions into; a mechanism to help her healing process. Carrie's anchor, her healing touchstone, was that she was happily married — she knew that she was loved and that there were no real skeletons in the closet, and that knowledge gave her peace.

The endings or 'deaths' of relationships can come in so many different forms. All are painful, all require a period of mourning, and all deserve acceptance and peace.

For me, acceptance and peace have been disrupted with waves of dismay, anguish and hurt. The last remaining waves in my otherwise calm sea of emotions have arisen from shining a light into the darkness of illusions I lived under for so long.

Connecting with yourself on a deep level helps you to see beyond the surface, beyond the superficial. Continuing to look for your truth is a great gift for your heart and your well-being. Allow the light within you to ignite and radiate. Shining the light of truth from your heart enables you to see clearly.

When you see what is happening around you and everything becomes clearer, emotions come up and some are not comfortable. This is a sign that you are growing beautifully.

The good news — the silver lining — is that, after the darkest nights come the dawn, the hope and the faith of a new day. To have the gift of self-love, self-awareness and self-compassion along with valuable insights is truly a blessing. To have the rest of your life ahead of you, free of the burden of illusion and access to new skills like a lighthouse warning you when you're in danger of crashing into the rocks of disillusion, is wondrous.

Find your truth

Loose boundaries often stem from a lack of self-worth or a sense that you must prove yourself. By putting down striving, trying and self-improvement, you can discover your truth. Permit yourself to recognise the truth of who you are underneath all the layers of expectations and burdens.

Ask yourself: "Who would I be and what would my life look like if I gave myself permission to live my truth?" Focus on your skills, gifts, strengths, wishes and dreams. If you feel called to share those gifts, trust that the right people will be drawn to you because of who you are.

You cannot be improved because you are already a masterpiece. Expressing yourself and creating the life you want is the path to living with ease. A life of comfort, lightness and inner peace.

Give yourself permission and the gift to live a life of ease.

A life where you stand in your truth, your power, and your strength.

And in doing so you will draw to you true friends and true reciprocal relationships.

Your energy and your truth are more important than manners. More important than attempting to please others. It's so important for you to make sure that your mental, emotional and social well-being is at the centre or the focus of your life. By making yourself a priority, Life and the Universe will reflect that choice back to you — drawing towards you experiences, opportunities and relationships where you are also a priority.

Conclusion

If you had told me a couple of years ago that the end of my marriage would open my heart and mind to new levels of self-acceptance and contentment, I wouldn't have believed you.

When I first met my ex-husband, my somewhat grey life became as vibrant as a double rainbow. The intense hues of love flooded over me, bringing extreme happiness. Yet, like rainbows and raindrops, our love evaporated, leaving me soaked in sadness as I grieved for the life I once had.

But what I initially saw as loss became an opportunity to reset my life — a blessing in disguise. This experience has gifted me with self-validation, confidence in who I am, and the rediscovery of beautiful parts of myself I had pushed aside.

As I reflect on my journey, I envision shoelaces being pulled together and tied in a bow. The threads of the past few years intertwining, much like when my children learned to tie their shoelaces. I still remember Molly's intense concentration as she carefully made the first loop, her frustration when she couldn't quite get it, and the pure delight on her face when she finally succeeded. That accomplishment opened new possibilities — more shoe options, no longer limited to velcro.

Much like Molly, I too have struggled, learned, and grown. A warm glow of pride fills my heart when I look back at how far I've come. The contrast between my thoughts and behaviours before my marriage ended and now is stark. The old me would often contract and crumble, shrinking under judgment, blame, and self-criticism. But today, I allow myself to expand. I invite curiosity, not judgment. Self-love and new perspectives enable me to grow, with a healthy dose of self-compassion to keep the weeds from overtaking the flowers.

I believe everything happens for a reason, even when the outcomes catch you off guard. Life's design holds lessons to embrace and gifts to receive. This beautiful, messy journey is one of self-discovery and growth. When guided by love, life places you on a path of deeper self-awareness, allowing you to live authentically and in your truth.

Be proud of yourself. Give yourself permission to walk with your head held high. Feel all your feelings — even on the days when tissues are necessary. Life is a journey, and every day is a school day. Take pride in not staying stuck, in embracing change, even when it's tough.

Before I go, I want to leave you with two questions to reflect on:

- ♥ If you knew they were never going to change, what would you do?
- ♥ What can you take away from change, instead of focusing on what change is taking away from you?

Amongst everything else I've taken away from my own change, the past year has brought a learning that deepened my self-discovery even further. After a friend's thoughtful suggestion a year ago, I embarked on the process of seeking an autism diagnosis. This diagnosis has been nothing short of a revelation — continuing my journey of self-love and connection. At first, the news shook me, but it soon brought deep validation and clarity, healing the wounds of misunderstanding, gaslighting, and rejection that had followed me for years.

One of the most profound realisations was that the biggest thing missing, especially in the later years of my marriage, was care. True care isn't transactional; it's not about what you contribute in economic terms, but about being valued simply for existing — imperfect and whole. In a genuinely supportive and caring environment where you can explore and grow at your own pace, you can thrive.

This diagnosis has opened new doors for me, and perhaps it will lead to another chapter — maybe even another book — where I explore this next part of my journey more deeply. After all, the story of self-discovery and healing never truly ends, and I'm excited to continue sharing what I uncover along the way.

As I look forward to my next chapter, I'm excited for yours as well.

With love and hugs

Lindsey x

Acknowledgements

I am truly blessed to have amazing family and friends around me who support and encourage my endeavours. Without the warm hugs, love, chocolate, late-night S.O.S calls and other various skill sets, this book would not have materialised. What started as a series of journal entries and stories transformed into a record of my journey, which I sincerely hope has helped or inspired you, dear reader, in some small way.

I thank you, the awesome person that holds this book in their hands, for picking it up and trusting that I had something of value to share with you. I'm sending you love and wish you all the peace and happiness in the world.

Huge thanks to Stacey Macdonald my Story Coach, who patiently and wisely teased out more emotion and depth from within me that I knew was possible. Thank you for expertly alchemising my thoughts into words, enabling me to share my truth and heal.

Much appreciation to Ceryn Rowntree for the incredible care you brought to editing my book. Your thoughtful attention to detail, gentle suggestions, and skillful polish helped my message truly shine. I'm deeply grateful for your expertise—and the heart you brought to every page.

Many thanks to Jean Haner for introducing me to the wonderful art of Nine Star Ki, and to Rex Lasselle, Michael Becherer and Alex and Danka Jack for deepening my knowledge and admiration for its transformative effects and applications.

Thank you to Nicola Humber and Em Mulholland at the Unbound Press for enabling me to experience what it truly feels like to be an author. To share my story and feel huge pride in seeing my book on bookshelves and in the hands of the people it resonates with is truly awesome.

The beautiful Nine Star Ki illustrations were created by my talented friend Lizzie Cairns of Blinkin' Imp; thank you, Petal. The lovely illustrations of Maya and Wendy were accurately and beautifully drawn by Gail Armstrong; many thanks to you.

Lynda Mangoro, for the front cover and interior design, my heartfelt gratitude. You listened to my vision and created something truly stunning that encapsulates both the essence of me and this book.

My family is my biggest joy and I am lucky to come from a line of strong women on both sides, many of whom enjoyed the art of storytelling. My beloved grandmother, Neta Charman was a beautiful poet; thank you for passing along the joy of writing.

To my mum for her unflinching love and support (and the occasional editing), you are my rock.

To my dad for the warm hugs and modelling maintaining kindness in adversity.

To Oliver and Molly, my heart bursts with love and pride in having the privilege to be your mum. Thank you for your patience whilst I wrote this book and rose from the ashes of our loss. I'm in awe at the incredible, warm, wise and courageous people you are. I love you to the moon and back.

About the Author

Lindsey Elms offers gentle, yet profound guidance on love and connection, teaching you to stand in your truth and follow your inner love song. She lives in beautiful Northumberland, UK with her family and fur babies.

With her writing, coaching and healing gifts, she leads women through a transformative experience of aligning them to their natural power and strengths. Weaving a path to empowerment, clarity and self-compassion through her encouraging conversational sessions.

Lindsey consults the ancient wisdom of Nine Star Ki, a foundational tool in her work. She has studied this insightful cosmology for over a decade and has been mentored by world-renowned teachers in this art.

Utilising her toolbox of alchemy, the author is skilled at creating a safe space for self-discovery and is a container for change. A great listener with a kind, open heart, and an intuition for potential, Lindsey gently inspires you to connect with your own inner peace, self-love and balance, especially during times of unexpected change, loss and grief.

Visit **lindseyelms.com** where you can book a Nine Star Ki reading or one-to-one coaching, and take the **Heart Gift Quiz** to discover your path to empowering relationships. Plus keep up to update with Lindsey's offerings and musings.

www.ingramcontent.com/pod-product-compliance
Ingram Content Group UK Ltd.
Pitfield, Milton Keynes, MK11 3LW, UK
UKHW052241300325
456766UK00005B/3